The Vision of Christ
By Marcus Clayton.

I dedicate this book to all the seekers out there looking for answers.

And I say unto you, ask, and it shall be given unto you;

Seek, and ye shall find; Knock and it shall be opened unto you.

For everyone that asketh receiveth; and he that seeketh findeth;

And to him that knocketh it shall be open.

Luke 11: 9 – 10

CONTENTS

ACKNOWLEDGEMENTS

I want to first give my honor and appreciation to my creator, the God of this universe. Then I want to honor the pastor and first lady of the church I was born into. Davis family, you have been my spiritual grandparents and you spirits live on with me every day. I then want to honor my newly found pastor and first lady the Purters.

I also want to honor all the pastors, sponsors and chaplains; I have come in contact with over the years. Then, lastly, I want to honor my mother, who gave me to God after my birth and has been here for me every step of the way.

I would like to acknowledge these guys for taking a part in putting this book together.

Main Editor: Christopher Bistryski
Spell Check: Marshawn Lawrence
Book Cover: Chevy
Story Sharer: Loony
The guy that encouraged me to write: Omez

INTRODUCTION

I am a God-fearing man, who was born again the summer of 2009. I was locked behind doors then and here it is now March 16, 2016. Well I am still behind closed doors, but my soul is free in Christ. I am still far from perfect, but in Jesus Christ I am forgiven of my sins, which is why I continually grow in Christ daily.

I was born and raised in Tacoma, Washington, Beginning life at a hospital by the name of Tacoma General. Oxygen had been cut off from my brain for 24 hours before my mother had an emergency C – section performed on her. I can honestly say that God has called me to his will and that he has had His hands on my life keeping me here before I was even born. When I look back on my life, I also see that the devil has tried to put me in situation after situation trying to take my life.

I grew up in a church family by the name of Genesis Baptist Church as the church family grew older and my pastor Freddy Davis grew old, he joined Genesis Church with a church family by the name of Living Worth, which has a much younger pastor by the name of Michael Purter.

I grew up in church, but I did not read, know, or truly follow the word of God until I was born again in a few months after being locked behind doors in 2009 and when. I began to see that the things my pastors had told me and not only told but showed me with their actions was truth.

I am currently facing 28 more years behind locked doors due to the fact that when I was of the world, I took a man's life while having a gun pressed up against my head. It does get hard from time to time, but when it's said and done, God loves me through everything, which is why I love him back by standing in his gift of grace, so that Jesus Christ can use my life to bring glory to the Father's name.

Thank you, Lord, FOR EVERY BREATH I TAKE!

Chapter 1

God Took A Crooked System and Changed Me.

I thought the truth would set me free. The truth was that the system, the world and the people around me, told lies, while I was trying so hard to keep it real amongst so much fake.

How could I have allowed my truth to be twisted around and used against me?

The system used my mistake and turned my woman against me in the courthouse of Pierce County Jail.

Did she tell the truth? No. Did she know she lied? I'm not sure, but the courts used her testimony to convict me of felony murder. After a two or three week trial. I was sentenced to 434 months in Washington State DOC (Dept. of Corrections that is).

I did not truly know that laws that the system of Washington State had put into effect, but while being locked up and reading up on the law, I see that by selling drugs I put myself in a situation that left me with no choice except to take a man's life or lose my own. At most I should have been charged with manslaughter, but because of the way the system works I was overcharged with a felony murder for a robbery that was never planned and never happened.

I believe I was overcharged to get scared into taking a deal for a smaller charge of murder in the 2 degree, which carried a sentence of 180 months. I prayed and prayed but did not take the deal for murder in the 2 degree. I decided

not to because after I read up on the laws of Washington State I realized that

what I had done was not capable of being a murder in the 2 degree.

However, I was found guilty according to a jury of 12 people who did not

know me, did not know the law, and who were quick to cast the first stone as if

they were perfect themselves.

I did not know what to do or how I was going to do it, but somehow, I

managed to trust God and leave everything in his hands, holding on to verses such

as:

Proverbs 3: 3 – 6, which says:

Let not mercy and truth forsake thee;

bind them about thy neck;

Write them upon the table of thine heart;

for so shalt thou find favor and good understanding

in the sight of God and man.

Trust unto thine Own understanding.

In all thy ways acknowledge him,

and he shall Direct thy paths.

Isaiah 54: 17 which says:

No weapon that is formed against thee shall prosper;

and every tongue that shall rise against thee in judgement

thou shalt condemn. This is the heritage of the servants of

the Lord, and their righteousness is of me, saith the Lord.

Those verses along with many more began to sink into my heart, which allowed God to begin his transformation in my life.

Romans 12: 2 Says:

> And be not conformed to this world: but be ye transformed by the renewing of your mind, that ye may prove what is that good and acceptable, and perfect, will of God.

The transformation that God has been doing within me has not happened overnight, but it has been happening through much hardship while holding on to his word. It has been about 8 years since this transformation within me has begun and to tell the truth my transformation is far from over, because I still battle the flesh daily. At this point I must stand strong in the word of God, and when growing weary, I must not faint, because I can do all things through Christ who strengthens me.

I constantly find myself thinking this is not my battle, but God's and it has already been won, by my Lord and Savior Jesus Christ. Do I get angry from time to time? Yes. But when I am angry I try my best to sit still and not react so that I can allow God the chance to move on my behalf.

I am always thankful, even when it hurts, because the knowledge of God lets me know that when it "hurts, I am being blessed" Matthew 5 : 3 – 12 lets me know all about what God is doing for me through hard and hurtful times. It says:

Blessed are the poor in spirit: for theirs is the Kingdom of Heaven.

Blessed are thy that mourn: for they shall be comforted.

Blessed are the meek: for they shall inherit the earth.

Blessed are they which do hunger and thirst after righteousness: for they shall be filled.

Blessed are the merciful: for they shall obtain mercy.

Blessed are the pure in heart: for they shall see God.

Blessed are the peacemakers; for they shall be called the Children of God. Blessed are those who are persecuted for righteousness sake: for theirs is the Kingdom of Heaven. Blessed are ye, when men shall revile you, and persecute you, and shall say all manner of evil against you falsely, for my sake. Rejoice, and be exceeding glad: for so persecuted they the prophets which were before you.

In those 9 verses God lets me know that no matter what may happen to me in life, even if the whole world rises up against me the only thing that can happen is that I will be blessed by Him as long as I do things his way.

It's all so simple, but at the same time it is very hard. I say that because it's a lot easier said than done when the flesh begins to rise. The biggest mistake that I make from time to time is taking situations into my own hands and thinking that I am the one that is right even when the truth is that I am truly wrong when I am thinking that way. Why? Because when I am doing things that way God's will is not being done in my life. In fact, when I am doing that, my actions are saying loudly!!! To God that 'I got control of this. I don't need your help right now. '

To be honest that is not only my mistake but that is the mistake nations and leaders of nations make, all the time, ever since the beginning of times.

In the Bible, the Book of Judges to be exact, a lot of evil was going on and in chapter 17: 6 plus chapter 21: 25 it clearly asks why there is so much evil.

Judges 17: 6 says, "In those days there was no king in Israel. But every man did that which was right in his own eyes."

And Judges 21:25 says, "In those days there was not king in Israel: every man did that which is right in his own eyes."

That just goes to show that when I or anybody else in this world does things the way they want to, instead of the way that Christ (who is the way, truth, and life) does it, then it only means one thing: they are only walking contrary to God's will. And when a man is walking contrary to the will of God, he is walking the ways of the world and the ways of the world belong to the father of all sin, which is Satan himself.

By having the fear of the Lord in my heart, it causes me to walk with God in God's will, which means I am walking by faith and not by sight. Because of that and what Christ did I am allowed to walk in God's Promises, which means I receive his blessings for myself and for my offspring for generations to come.

The word lets me know about the blessings God gives to me when I am walking with him.

In Leviticus 26: 3 – 9 it says:

> If ye walk in my statues and keep my commandments, and
> do them; then I will give you rain in due season, and the trees
> of the field shall yield their fruit.
> And your threshing shall reach unto the vintage,
> and the vintage shall reach unto the sowing time:
> and ye shall eat your bread to the full, and dwell in your land safely.
> And I will give peace in the land. And ye shall lie down and non
> shall make you afraid: and I will rid evil beasts out of the land,
> neither shall the sword go through your land.
> And ye shall chase your enemies, and they shall fall before you
> by the sword.
> And five of you shall chase an hundred, and an hundred of you
> shall put ten thousand to flight: and your enemies shall
> fall before you by the sword
> For I will have respect unto you, and make you fruitful and
> multiply you and establish my covenant with you.

Then a little deeper in that chapter God makes it clear what will happen to any and everybody who is contrary to him.

Leviticus 26: 23 – 30 says this:

> And if ye will not be reformed by me by these things, but will
> walk contrary unto me;
> Then will I also walk contrary unto you, and will punish you
> yet seven times for your sins.

And I will bring a sword upon you, that shall avenge the quarrel

of my covenant: and when ye are gathered together within

your cities, I will send the pestilence among you; and ye shall

be delivered into the hand of the enemy.

And when I have broken the staff of your bread, ten women

shall bake your bread in one oven, and they shall deliver

you your bread again by weight: and ye shall eat, and not

be satisfied.

And if ye will not for all of this hearken unto me, but walk

contrary unto me;

Then I will walk contrary unto you also in fury; and I, even

I will chastise you seven times for your sins.

And ye shall eat the flesh of your sons and the flesh of

your daughters shall ye eat.

And I will destroy your high places, and cut down your images,

and cast your carcasses upon the carcasses of your idols,

and my soul shall abhor you.

All in all my spirit is so vexed about the way this system is set up and I can only imagine how deceived the person is who is in charge of the way everything is run. The truth is, when it's all said and done there is only one who is in charge of it all and that one is my Lord and Savior Jesus Christ. He has by all means used this crooked system to change my heart and save my soul from eternal damnation with the one and only true enemy, Satan himself

Chapter 2
Will You Give Your Soul for the World,

Or live Forever with Jesus Christ

1 John 2: 15 – 18 says:

> Love not the world, neither the things that are in the world.
>
> If any man love the world, the love of the father is not in him.
>
> For all that is in the world, the lust of the flesh, and the lust of
>
> the eyes, and the pride of life, is not of the father,
>
> but is of the world.
>
> And the world passeth away, and the lust thereof:
>
> but he that doeth the will of God abideth forever.
>
> Little children, it is the last times: and as ye have heard
>
> that antichrist shall come, even now are there many
>
> antichrists; whereby we know that it is the last time...

It can be easy to fall into the ways of the world then get left behind when Christ comes back. Are your desires to please Christ or to please those who are of the world?

When looking at life from a worldly view, it seems as if there are so many things to do, things to accomplish, and so many places to go. The only thing is that there's only a lifetime to get everything done. Because of this, humans get to where they think they want to be, but yet they're never satisfied. Not only are humans never satisfied, they never seem to go further than where they are, or they get caught up in living the fast life and in doing so they seem to stop caring for others. Humans also find themselves living life doing the same things over and over again while expecting different results.

I'm here to let you know that living life with Christ defeats all the worldly misery that humans are born into and must otherwise face and look forward to. For starters humans begin to look forward to eternal life, instead of death, they get to look forward to growing in Christ with every breath they take. Humans will never get to a certain point in life, then stop, no matter if the situation is what they were striving for nor if it's something that is just too much to bear.

Living life with Jesus Christ is the answer for everything. Why??? Because Jesus Christ has already answered to everything humans can possibly go through in life. Jesus is the strength when humans are weak, Jesus is the refuge when they need shelter, Jesus is always there giving love, even when no one else is. Jesus is the strong tower, the rock that the builders rejected, Jesus came to this world, born at the bottom and rose back to the top. The world was saved through Jesus Christ, but yet the world was against him.

Jesus Christ did what he did for humans because of the love God has for humankind and God wants humans to live life instead of being an existence. John 3:16 says, "For God so loved the world, that he gave his only begotten son, that whosoever believeth in him should not perish, but have everlasting life." Jesus Christ gives humans an unbreakable joy, love, peace, and kindness. Jesus is God's love, mercy, favor, and hope.

Galatians 5: 22 – 23 says, "But the fruit of the spirit is love, joy, peace, long suffering, gentleness, goodness, faith, meekness temperance: against such there is no law…" When chasing the ways of the world, humans may find love, joy, peace, and kindness but those things will never last forever, because they are only temporary. When humans choose the ways of the world it is as if they praise the creation instead of the creator who created the creation in the first place.

Galatians 5: 19 – 21 says:

> Now the works of the flesh are manifest, which are these;
> Adultery, fornication, uncleanness, lasciviousness, Idolatry,
> Witchcraft, hatred, variance, emulations, wrath, strife, seditions,
> Heresies, envying, murders, drunkenness, revellings, and suchlike:
> Of the which I tell you in time past, that they which do such things
> Not inherit the Kingdom of God…

When living in the worldly ways, humans tend to do evil things all the time without knowing the wrong that they are doing. Humans also tend to take their own lives when they are of the and things go bad. Humans usually do that because they have no clue about how valuable their lives are, plus they never get that chance to find out why they were given life in the first place.

When living life in Christ humans know that life and all situations that may come, all have purpose because everything in this world has one purpose. That purpose is Jesus Christ.

John 1: 1 – 3 says:

> In the beginning was the word, and the word was with God,
> and the word was God.
> The same was in the beginning with God.

All things were made by Him and without him was not anything made that was made.

It was by one man that sins entered the world and it is one man who washes sins away. There is no way around sin inn this world except through Jesus Christ because humans are all born into a world of sin. Jesus Christ is the Sinner's Savior, the Prince of peace and the Breastplate of Righteousness.

People in the world only treat people right when they are doing good in life, but when someone is down and out, people seem to kick them time after time, to keep them down. It doesn't matter how good a person does after messing up, people still bring the wrong up to try tearing that person down.

When living in Christ, it doesn't matter how many times a person trips and falls because Jesus is always there to pick them back up. Jesus does that since believers are forgiven through God's Gift of Grace, which is Jesus Christ. Believers are forgiven over and over again. God's Word says that they should be forgiven 70 x 7 times.

John 14:6 says, "Jesus saith unto him, I am the way, the truth and the life: no man cometh unto the father, but by me. "Jesus makes it very clear that he is the way and that there is no way to God except through him.

The world says in God we trust, but all the worldly actions prove over and over again that most humans don't truly trust in God. The word of God lets humans know that as a believer they should live in the world but not be of the world. By doing that, not only would they live forever, God would be able to use them to bring others to Christ as well.

When humans are of the world, they never give or experience real love, because worldly love always fails when it doesn't get what it wants in return. The love of Christ is real because Jesus is the Son of God and God is love, so throughout all of his ways God is loving humans, even when he is telling us to something or not to do something.

God told Adam and Ever that they could eat from any tree in the garden, except for one. He told Adam and Eve those things out of love. But because of the fact that they disobeyed God, they hurt themselves along with the rest of humankind.

Before the disobedience of Adam, man ruled the world and everything in it. But because of the fact that Adam disobeyed God, Satan stole Adam's blessing. Now Satan rules the world except for those who are in Jesus Christ.

Jesus Christ gave his life to make a way for humankind by obeying God so that they can overcome their sinful nature through his forgiveness. Being in the world and not of the world is not an easy thing to do, but God's word is true: we can do all things through Christ who gives us strength. Philippians 4:13 says, "I can do all things through Christ which strengthened me. "

When humans go through hardships in life while depending on Jesus Christ to provide them with the strength, they need to make it through, it's always more than worth it in the end. It's just the way things work in life: anything that is good for a person is never easy to overcome, or should I say achieve Hard work always pays off in the end, In fact the harder a person works the better the end results. The more a human goes through while surrendering all to Jesus Christ, the stronger Christ gets within a person's life.

If Jesus Christ is in a human's life, it does not mean that they're not going to suffer; it does mean that their suffering will not be in vain.

Romans 8: 16 – 19 says:

> The spirit itself beareth witness with our spirit,
>
> that we are the children of God:
>
> And if children, then heirs; heirs of God, and joint –
>
> heirs with Christ; if so be that we suffer with him,
>
> that we may also be glorified together.
>
> For I reckon that the sufferings of this present time are
>
> not worthy to be compared with the glory which shall
>
> be revealed in us.
>
> For the earnest expectation of the creature waiteth
>
> for the manifestation of the Sons of God.

When being a part of the world, humans will still suffer, but the suffering that a human may go through without Jesus Christ will have no purpose at all.

Everyone here on this earth has been born into this world of sin and on top of that they have taken on some kinds of worldly characteristics. A lot of the worldly ways harden the heart of humans through all the suffering humans go through in everyday life. When humans open their hearts to Jesus Christ, Jesus comes in and begins to clean, heal, and build their hearts into the image that they were truly created to be.

Prayer

Lord Heavenly Father, I come to you in the Name of Jesus, opening my heart to let Jesus Christ in, so he can begin the cleaning, healing, and rebuilding process. My life belongs to you and I thank you for your love.

In Jesus Name, Amen.

Chapter 3

Living in Christ While Being Around

People Who Are of the World

Galatians 5: 16 – 17 says:

> This I say then, walk in the spirit, and ye shall
> not fulfill the lust of the flesh. For the flesh lusteth
> against the spirit, and the spirit against the flesh:
> and these are contrary the one to the other: so that ye
> cannot do the things that ye would.

As a believer following Christ, a person tends to have a harder time doing so when they are around other humans who are of the world. The reason is simple. It's because those people who are of the world are doing things in the flesh and those who are in Christ are walking in the spirit. Well, the spirit and the flesh do not agree on doing the same things. That's because the spirit and the flesh take on two completely different roles.

The works for the flesh are: Adultery, Uncleanness, Lewdness, Fornication, Sorcery, Hatred, Idolatry, Contentions, Jealousies, and Selfish ambitions, Outbursts of wrath, Dissensions, Envy, Drunkenness, Revelries, and Murders. While on the other hand, the fruits of the spirit are: Love, Joy, Peace, long-suffering, Kindness, Goodness, Faithfulness, Gentleness, and Self – Control. The two are totally different from one another. The spirit is of the light and the flesh is of darkness.

If the people of the world are in the dark and those who are in Christ are in the light, then either the people who are in the world will come to the light or those who are in Christ can fall back into the ways of the flesh. Humans who are in Christ may even face persecution as Christ did just to give the opportunity for people who are of the world to know the truth, which is Jesus Christ.

Jesus Christ is in everything that humans can possibly think of and Jesus came to this world of darkness to be the light. Not only did Jesus come to be the light, but since he died for humankind his light shines through all that walk in the spirit through worldly persecution while walking with Christ.

Humans must understand that while trying to bring others to Christ, by being a witness, and doing it on their own strength, they can find their selves reacting to some situations in the flesh instead of in the spirit. But when people are truly walking in the word of God, they are allowing Christ to witness through them.

When a person who is of the world is around people who are living in Christ they might not accept Christ into their heart right then and there. When they do, Jesus will bring to remembrance the people in their past who allowed Christ to be a witness through them.

These are some of the ways that God works. God works in these ways because he is a loving patient God who knows when, where and how he is going to open a human's spiritual eyes so they can see and understand his ways.

Matthew 5: 14 – 16 says:

> Ye are the light of the world. A city that is set on
>> an hill cannot be hid.
>
> Neither do men light a candle,
>> and put it under a bushel, but on a candlestick;
>>
>> and it giveth light unto all that are in the house.
>
> Let your light so shine before men, that they may see
>> your good works, and glorify your Father,
>>
>> which is in heaven.

When allowing the light of Jesus Christ to shine through a human, that human cannot let the light that is within them be hidden. The people who are of the world only know of Christ, but those people do not truly live in Christ by allowing Christ to live through them.

The word of God lets people know that if they say they know Jesus but on the other hand do not truly walk in Christ, then when the day of judgement comes, Jesus Christ will not know those who did not truly know his ways. The word of God also lets humans know that when they have the light of Jesus Christ dwelling within them, they must not let the light be hidden, since the light of Jesus Christ is here to bring light into the darkness of this world and the people who are of the world are trapped in the darkness of the world without knowing that they are or they have known nothing else and believe whole heartedly that the things they do are right.

Every time that a follower of Jesus Christ allows the light to shine through them, it gives another person who is not truly a believer the opportunity to step out of the darkness of the world and into the light of Jesus Christ. This is why it is so very important for true believers to live life in the light of Jesus Christ while being around those who are lost in the darkness of the world.

A lot of times a true believer can be a witness of the light to their closest loved ones who are living in the darkness of the world. The true believer can also fall into hiding the light of Jesus Christ by loving their loved ones more than they love God. When allowing the light of Jesus Christ to shine, it gives Jesus Christ the power to take control and overcome the darkness once again.

Humans must remember as often as possible that they need nobody else in life more than they need God and His will. Sometimes people hurt themselves by loving others who don't want to be loved or who are afraid to be loved and love back. When being around people who are of the world and letting the light of Jesus Christ shine, there is a strong possibility that the one who is allowing the light of Jesus Christ to shine will get left out because they don't want to do the things that the people who are of the world want to do. But as a true believer, who is allowing Jesus Christ to live, they know that the person who is in the light is never really alone or left out because God is with them 24 hours of each day and the people of the world may be the ones who get left out when its all said and done.

This does not mean that true believers should look at themselves as being better than those people who are of the world. But it does mean that true believers should stay strong in Christ, let Jesus shine and bring others to Christ through actions of surrendering all.

John 1: 4 – 14 says:

In him was life; and the life was the light of men.
And the light shineth in darkness; and the darkness comprehended it not.
There was a man sent from God, whose name was John.

The same came from a witness, to bear witness of the light, that all men through him might believe. He was not that light, but was sent to bear witness of that light.

That was that true light, which lighteth every man that cometh into the world.

He was in the world, and the world was made by him, and the world knew him not. He came unto his own, and his own received him not.

But as many as received him, to them gave the power to become the sons of God, even to them that believe on his name, which were born not of blood nor of the will of the flesh, nor of the will of man, but of God.

And the word was made flesh, and dwelt among us and we beheld his glory, the glory as of the only begotten of the Father full of grace and truth.

The true light is Jesus Christ.

Chapter 4

All things were made for Christ

John 1: 1 – 3 says;

> In the beginning was the word, and the word was with God,
>
> and the Word was God.
>
> The same was in the beginning with God.
>
> All things were made by him and without him was not
>
> anything made that was made.

Jesus can use humans along with everything they have done and been through in their past. It does not matter who a person is, what they have done or where they are at in life, Jesus Christ can and will use them as long as they allow him to.

In the word of God Is states that Jesus Christ came to save the humans who were lost. Jesus came to save tax collectors, murderers, harlots, adulterers, and thieves.

In the word of God which is the bible, humans have been doing all of these things in life and that's because those things are a part of human nature, which is sin.

But when the humans who wrote the word or who were in the word truly accepted Jesus Christ in their hearts and lives, they began to make a change not only in their life, but in other people's lives as well. Paul is a man of the word who has wrote multiple book in the Bible, such as Romans; 1 and 2, Corinthians, Galatians, Ephesians, Philippians, Colossians; 1 and 2, Thessalonians; 1 and 2, Timothy , Titus, and Philemon, which were written while he was a prisoner of Rome.

Paul was a man who practiced the law before he truly allowed Jesus Christ to live through him. Paul was a persecutor of the Jews, but when Jesus Christ began to live through him, the Jews who were once persecuted by Paul for breaking the law, truly witnessed the change that Christ had done within Paul. The most important thing that Paul did was ask Christ to live through him instead of trying to follow the word on his own strength.

God wants to do the same thing for the rest of humankind as he did for Paul and all the rest of the mighty men and women of God. The only thing humans need to do is give everything they have, have done, have gone through, and are going through to God so Christ can use it to glorify the Father. The hardest part for humans to do is to accept that they are constantly wrong and that they cannot live righteously on their own.

For a human to allow Jesus Christ to live through them is God's will being done in their life and when Christ is living through humans, God the Father only sees them as the light. Jesus is the light and he outshines any darkness that is within humankind, which is why God the Father only sees his only begotten son Jesus Christ when he looks at humans who are allowing Christ to live. It is an amazing thing how Jesus Christ can let the Father use the most ugliest things that humans have been through, have done to others, or have done to themselves to glorify his name, but only if humans allow him to.

All throughout the Gospels of the Bible (Matthew, Mark, Luke, and John) Jesus Christ speaks of being about his Father's business and with everything Jesus Christ did he was glorifying God the Father. When humans allow Jesus Christ to use them, Jesus will also glorify the Father through them allowing God to do what he has promised, which is to bless those who are of the faith of Jesus Christ. These blessing that are being spoken of are ones that humans would not believe unless Christ was alive during the miracles of the Father through them. Not only will God do miracles for the saints, but he will also do them for the worst of the worst.

A lot of people say that they have done too much wrong for them to give their life to God and live a good life now, but that is a lie from the pits of hell because Jesus Christ died so that humans could be washed in is blood. Through Jesus Christ humans can be cleansed as white as snow and they are no longer covered in stains from their past. The thing that humans should always remember is that God not only forgives but most importantly he forgets. That is why it does not matter what humans do, good or bad, because there is nothing they can do to change God's ways. Either they are walking with Christ, or not.

Jesus Christ is the one who has already done what God has planned to be done for humankind. The only thing is that humans will never find out what God wants to do through them unless they ask Jesus Christ to come into their life and show them the way. When they allow Christ to live through them then everything that they have been through, or are going through or will go through, will be the will of God being done in their life. Jesus Christ was sent to us to lead the way as an example and his will was always the Father's. So we should follow that example and let him live through us.

When standing in the will of God they begin to stand in the promises of God, they begin to stand in the promises of God and one of the promises that God made was one to Abraham. God promised to Abraham that he would bless him along with all of his descendants. The word of God lets humans know that they are all descendants of Abraham through true faith in the Son of God, Jesus Christ. But faith is something more than saying I believe in Jesus Christ. Faith is more of an action that shows belief through a human walk of following Christ. This is the very reason why if a person says they have faith in Jesus Christ but then does not allow him to live through them they are only being deceived.

In James 2: 14 – 24 it says:

> What does it profit, my brethren, though a man says he hath
> faith, and have not works? Can faith save him?
> If a brother or sister be naked and destituts of daily food,
> and one of you say unto them, depart in peace, be ye
> warmed and filled; not withstanding ye give them those
> things which are needful to the body; what doth it profit?
> Even so faith if it hath not works, is dead, being alone.
> Yes a man may say, thou hast faith, and I have works:
> show me thy faith without thy works, and I will show
> thee my faith by my works. Thou believest that there is one God;
> though doest well: the devils also believe, and tremble.
> But wilt thou know, oh vain man, that faith without works

is dead? Was not Abraham our father justified by works,

when he had offered Isaac his son upon the altar?

Seest though how faith wrought with his works,

and by works was faith made perfect? And the scripture

was fulfilled which saith, Abraham believed God and

it was imputed unto him for righteousness: and he was

called the friend of God.

Ye see then how that by works a man is justified and by faith only.

Everyone Stumbles

Humans all fall short of God's Glory. The word of God states that when people break any of the 10 commandments, which were given to Moses, they break all 10. When humans break the law, they become sinners and when living in sin the punishment for sin is death. But God loves so much that although humans sin against him he sent his only begotten son, so that people can have a way to sin no more.

One of the biggest things that humans must understand is that they are not any better than the next person, no matter what kind of mistakes that person or the next person has made in life. This is because sin is sin in God's eye no matter what it is. All humans can do is seek God for mercy and forgiveness through all of their sins.

When humans hold onto what the next person has done to them, instead of allowing Christ to forgive that person through them, then they are not only hurting the person that they don't forgive, but they are hurting themselves even more. Because they are holding onto hate in their hearts instead of holding onto Jesus Christ.

Forgiving other people is not an easy thing to do and a person forgiving themselves is even harder. A lot of times people say they forgive, but they do not truly forgive who they say they forgive. Truly forgiving a person starts in prayer. A human should ask God to heal their heart through the lashes that Jesus Christ took to heal the brokenhearted and then they should ask Christ to truly forgive through them the person who wronged them.

When humans try to forgive on their own strength they can never truly forgive. Anything a human does is wrong. It does not matter if they think its's good or bad in the first place because the only thing that is going to please God is if humans allow Jesus Christ to use whatever it is to glorify the Father. If humans are not giving God the glory for everything, they are only being prideful and they are seeking self – righteousness.

When humans are not living in the spirit of Jesus Christ, they are in the flesh and the flesh is weak because the flesh reacts on what others think, what it sees and what it hears. If the flesh wants to kill, steal, do drugs, have sex or whatever else it wants to do, the flesh is going to do it, unless the spirit of God is overpowering the flesh. This is the very reason why Jesus Christ steps to the lowest point of this world in the flesh to overcome everything and give humankind the chance to receive the Holy Spirit of God.

Just remember humans will all stumble and most of the time they will stumble over the same things over and over again. But Jesus Christ died, and rose again, so that humans can be forgiven and truly seek his ways instead of their own ways.

Why Jesus Can Use Everything

Jesus Christ is ruler over everything, even Satan along with everything he tries to do. From time to time it seems as if Satan is winning, but through faith humans can know that Satan can never ever defeat God's will, which is Jesus Christ and that's because Jesus uses everything Satan means for evil for good. Satan causes pain and sorrow, but since Christ overcome, all Satan can do is allow God to strengthen hearts.

Satan might think he is winning, but the truth is that Jesus Christ is always there with the upper hand. That is why it does not matter about what humans have done wrong or right, all that matters is that humans allow Jesus Christ to use it to glorify the Father.

Jesus Christ can use anybody, what they have done or have been through to save another humans life. Jesus can use one person's life to save another person or he can use that one person to save millions. So that is another reason why it's so important for humans to allow Jesus Christ to live through them and use everything that they go through, even in the times when they stumble over their own selfish ways.

Colossians 1: 16- 20 says:

For by him were all things created, that are in heaven, and that are in earth, visible and invisible, whether they be thrones, or dominions, or principalities, or powers: all things were created by him and for him. And he is before all things, and by him all things consist. And he is the head of the body, the church: who is the beginning the first born from the dead; that in all things he might have the preeminence. For it pleased the Father that in him should all fullness dwell; and, having made peace through blood of his cross, by him to reconcile all things unto himself; by him, I say, whether they be things in earth, or things in heaven.

Chapter 5

Let Christ Have the Wheel

I once read a story that goes like this. There was a young man newly out if high school and undecided about what to do with his life. Go to college or university? Perhaps so. But what would he want to study? And how would he pay for such education. He decided to travel, wander wherever his whims would lead, and see what ideas would come to him.

One day when he was in New York City he decided to go to the top of the Empire State Building and see the view. On the way up the elevator, he stopped on the 77th floor. A man stepped into the elevator. He was all – powerful – looking and all dressed in white.

As the elevator elevated toward the top floor they talked, and the young man mentioned that he was travelling while deciding what do with his life. The man in white said, "There is this distant city that you should look into." As he described this distant city it sounded truly wonderful. The young man asked, "how far?" The man in white said, "About 105 trillion miles." But still the young man was interested and intrigued by what he had heard about the distant city.

The elevator arrived at the top of the building and the view was well worth the effort. Later, back in the elevator and on the way down, the young man was still thinking about the distant city. When the elevator stopped at the 66th floor, another very tall and impressive man stepped in.

He was all dressed in black and there was certain intensity about him. As the elevator continued down, they talked, and the young man mentioned the distant city. The man in black smiled and said, "I too have a city." He told of the lights, oh the lights, and fun! He told of drinks and food galore, shows, great weather, swimming pools, lots to see and explore. The young man asked, "How far?" The man in black said, you can be there in a matter of hours. So, the young man decided to go see fun city.

It was fun, busy, and fast and furious. But in a few days the young man was tired and out of money and he had discovered that the fun just did not last. It was all so self – centered and repetitive. And he still could not get that distant city, and the way the man in white had talked about it, out of his mind.

He was able to get a car that would go far and fast and began trying to find the road to the distant city. Soon he found a road with a road sign that said, "Distant City, 105 trillion miles." 'Well,' he thought, 'If you are going that far you need to go at least 100 miles an hour.' And away he went.

But soon something became very clear. Most of the cars were going in the opposite direction from Distant City and many of them were going really fast. It was not easy to avoid a head – on crash. And it was hard to go 100 mph against traffic. Soon he found himself driving on the shoulder. He found his speed going down. But occasionally he was able to make pretty good time.

One day as he was making good time, he saw a huge diesel truck coming straight for him. It seemed to speed up and ran him right into the ditch. This happened to him often. As soon as he began to make reasonable time up the road one of the huge trucks would run him off the road. And the driver was always laughing. He was not making very good progress toward Distant City.

One day he was sitting in a ditch after being ran off the road by the diesel truck, and he was feeling discouraged. He was sitting with his head on the wheel and thinking about giving up, turning around and going with the flow of traffic. But then he heard a tap – tap- tap on the car window. He looked to see the man in white, just outside the window. He rolled down the window and says, "Wow! Where did you come from? It's good to see you again!"

The man in white smiled and said, "Do you want me to drive? The young man was still surprised and wondering if this was real. The man in white looking at him intently and said again, "Do you want me to drive? I've been over the road." The young man thought, 'He must know the way to Distant City. He's been over the road before and I'm certainly not doing so well on my own.' Then the young man made a decision, a very important decision. He moved over, out of the driver's seat and gave control to the man white.

Now the man in white was driving. They pulled out into traffic and headed right up the middle road at 100 mph. The other cars steered clear and they were flying along toward Distant City. He was thrilled with his driver. He even wanted bumper stickers saying, "Honk if you know my Driver." He could talk to his driver and his driver told him about Distant City. As he was driving his sleeve fell back on his arm and it was as big muscular arm. He asked what he does for a living, and he said he is a carpenter.

They were making wonderful progress and then it happened. Looking ahead he sees one of the huge diesel trucks loaded with logs. It made no difference who was driving, the truck headed straight for them. The driver did not seem to notice. He asked him, "Do you see the Truck?" "Yes," he said, sounding unconcerned. He looked at the truck, then the driver. He could not stand it. The truck was getting too close. At the last instant he grabbed for the wheel and the driver let him have it because he could have the wheel at any time…. This time the car goes into the ditch at 100 mph. After the dust settles, he looked over at the driver and the driver looked at him. "Do you want me to drive again?" the driver asked. "Yes," he said. But the fenders were all bent in against the tires. Not only was the driver a carpenter he was also a great body and fender man and soon they were back on the road.

He told himself that his driver had already been over the road before, so he must know about diesel trucks. He knew he needed to trust him to do the driving. Soon enough it happened again. Another truck, with three trailers all loaded, was headed straight for them. He looked at the driver who looked completely unconcerned. In fact, he noticed that the driver stepped up the speed to 110 mph, staying calm. But he was no longer calm.

He fastened he seat belt. Then he unfastened it. He wanted to take the wheel again, but instead he sat on his hands. At the last second the truck went into the ditch. Just before the truck crashed, he got a good look at the truck driver. He had a pitchfork with him in the cab, 'probably for loading hay, 'he thought but he was not laughing! It had taken every ounce of strength and effort he had to keep his hands off of the wheel and to let his driver control the situation. This trust thing is not easy. He asked his driver about it and his driver said the guidebook calls it a fight; the fight of faith and it is about the hardest thing for a natural born human to learn to do.

He could not explain how it happened but one day he found himself behind the wheel with his driver over in the passenger's seat. At first, he was uneasy and almost mentioned it to the driver. But then he reasoned: he has seen his driver drive; his driver is right there with him; he should be able to do it just like his driver. So, he continued to control the car on his own. It does not take long before he saw it in the distance, a hugs diesel truck. It looked like a double – trailer oil tanker and it was coming really fast.

He kept driving straight. He even stepped the speed up a little to about 101 mph. The truck was getting close. He closed his eyes and there was a truly terrible head – on collision. He would have been killed instantly except for one thing. At the last instant, his driver threw himself between him and the steering wheel and he took the hit for him.

The wreck was in the ditch. His driver was bleeding and bruised, but he was conscious, and he said to him, "Do you want me to drive?" "Drive what?" he asked. There were mangled parts of the car all over the road. But he found out that there was nothing too hard for his driver.

Soon the driver had it all back together again and they were back on the road making great time Distant City. He kept looking at his driver. His driver had the marks of the wreck still on him. He apologized for being so dense and he asked his driver to forgive him and his driver did of course. His driver said the important thing is to stay on the road.

Currently, they are making good progress toward Distant City and lately he had been feeling less anxious about getting to the city and more content with just being with his driver. There is no end to the interesting things his driver talks about and the more he understood the more fun he was having.

Proverbs 3: 5 – 7 says, "Trust in the Lord with all thine heart; and lean not unto thine own understanding. In all thy ways acknowledge him, and he shall direct thy paths. Be not wise in thine own eyes: fear the lord and depart from evil."

In the story the man in white represents Jesus Christ and the young man represents humans as being followers of Christ. The man in black represents Satan. Distant City represents the Kingdom of God. Fun City, with lights and food, represents the worldly pleasures that humans can receive with hardly any effort. The traffic coming in the opposite way represents the worldly humans, who Satan uses to try and stop true believers from inheriting the Kingdom of God.

The most important part of the story was the fact that the young man learned how to trust in the lord with all his heart. Believers who follow Jesus Christ always seem to keep trying to grab hold of the wheel whenever times get hard in life instead of letting Jesus Christ do what he does best. Humans also give the wheel to Jesus, but then they get scared at the last second turning off the road when they think they are going to crash.

Another thing that humans do is trust Jesus to have control of the wheel, but then one day they think they can do what they have seen Jesus do on their own. When humans take control and think they can do it on their own, they ten to crash and put their own life in danger, just like the young man did in the story.

Humans must wake up every morning thanking God and asking Jesus Christ to take the wheel so that God's will can be done in their life.

The word of God lets people know that they must pick up their cross and follow Jesus Christ daily. Not just every once in a while, but every single second of each day. If not, humans begin to take ahold of the wheel and when doing that they are only trying to control their life with their own strength, instead of doing things through Christ.

Jesus Christ is everywhere all at the same time, but when humans are controlling the wheel, they are only keeping Jesus Christ in the passenger seat of their car. When they crash Jesus tends to shield them and they end up hurting Christ. It is as if they are the ones who drive the nails through his hands and feet.

That is because Jesus got upon the cross to forgive the sins of humankind, not for himself or for people to just remember him. He did it so that he could live through each and every human so that he can overcome their sinful nature for them. Now that Jesus Christ did what God needed to do to save humankind, all people need to do now is reach out grab hold of Christ and let him control the wheel.

There are many things that humans face in life that they want to have control of. They have people in their life that they think they have control of, but there is no truth in that. If humans are trying to be in control or they think they are in control, they are only driving on the shoulder and they are bound to drive themselves along with everybody else they are trying to control off in the ditch.

When Jesus Christ is in control he is in control of every person, place or thing in a person's life. And where he is going to Distant City, which is heaven and everything a person wants is going to be there.

Matthew 25: 31 – 34 says:

> When the Son of Man shall come in His glory, and all the
> holy angels with him, then shall he sit upon the throne of
> his glory: And before him shall be gathered all nations:
> And he shall separate them one from another, as a
> shepherd divideth his sheep from the goats: And he
> shall set the sheep on his right hand, but the goats on the left.
> Then shall the king say unto them on his right hand,
> come, yes blessed of my father, inherit the Kingdom
> prepared for you from the foundation of the world.

Chapter 6

Satan is the Enemy

1 John 3: 8 – 12 says:

> He that comitteth sin is of the devil, for the devil
> sinneth from the beginning. For this purpose, the Son
> of God was manifested, that he might destroy the works
> of the devil. Whosoever is born of God doth not commit sin;
> for his seed remaineth in him: and he cannot sin,
> because he is born of God. In this the children of God
> are manifest, and the children of the devil: whosoever
> doeth not righteousness is not of God, neither he that
> loveth not his brother. For this is the message that ye
> heard from the beginning, that we should love on another.
> Not as Cain, who was of the wicked one, and
> slew his brother. And wherefor slew he him?
> Because his own works were evil, and his brother's
> righteous.

Satan did not bow to Christ because of pride and pride always comes before the fall. Satan knows the consequences for the choice that he has made. He knows that his time is near, which is why Satan wants to trick humans into selling their soul for the world and in doing that they will follow the devil to his destination. If you are reading this book right now, you do know where Satan's destination is and that his destination is hell.

Satan is truly mad, because of the choice that he had mad, wanting to be God himself. But there is only one God, which God works in threes: Father, Spirit, and Son. Satan's pride is allowing him to think that he is the God of this world. But there is no way that he can truly be who he thinks he is because everything Satan has to give is stolen and how can he be God of something that, on, he did not create, and , two, God is only allowing him to have. Because of the fact that Satan has stolen everything, he thinks he is God, which goes to show that what he has is not his and it will be given back to the rightful owner sooner or later.

Satan can, will, and wants to hurt God by hurting humankind, but the only way that Satan can hurt humans is if they allow him to. Satan knows that the only way he cannot hurt a human is if they are walking in Christ and Christ in them. When humans walk in Christ, they are promised that everything Satan can do to try getting them to turn on God only helps them become stronger in Christ. Satan knows that Jesus Christ will win every battle. But the one that Satan is really worried about is the final battle, when he loses everything and has no choice except to bow before Jesus Christ.

Satan knows God's ways even better than all humans, which is why he can and will take the word of God then twist it around to say it is contradicting or lie and say it is saying to do something that God is not really wanting a human to. For example Satan knows that God loves humankind so much that he gives humans a free will and for that reason God will not take from human kind unless they are going to love him enough to trust giving their life to him so that Jesus Christ can overcome Satan. This is the reason why Satan does everything in his power to keep humans from getting closer to God.

Satan uses things like drugs, money, for males' females and for females' males to keep humans away from Go. Satan even goes as far as same sex relations to keep humans away from their true creator. Satan knows that he can only hurt God by hurting humans. God loves every human the same and every time a human sin they sin against God. And they hurt God because they hurt themselves.

Satan is very deceptive, and the words of God lets humans know that Satan came to steal, kill, and destroy. The truth is this: Satan is going to steal, kill and destroy if humans are not walking in Christ. Satan will turn humans against other humans. He will kill a person who is close to someone else. He will give people money and respect the wrong way then turn around and steal it back. He will take love then turn it to hate and Satan will try to do whatever he needs to do take a person's life when they are not walking with Jesus Christ. If someone is walking with Christ Satan will do that entire he can't to stop that person from walking with Christ.

Satan does the things that he does in the dark. It is because he wants no one to see the things he does. But God does and brings everything to the light including Satan's evil ways.

When humans are trying to be nice to others and then others take their kindness for weakness, it is because Satan is using those people to try stopping them from doing things the God wants them done. When humans are handling things in a negative manner it seems as if Satan does not attack them as hard as he does when they are doing things God's. Satan does that when humans are doing things God's way because he knows that the Kingdom of God is growing and if God's Kingdom growing that means Satan is getting smaller. When humans are not doing things God's way they are walking contrary to his word and that means Satan has control of their actions and when Satan has control of humans' actions, those people are the ones that tend to take someone's kindness for weakness

God's ways are so strong that his weakness is stronger than any human's or demon's strength and because of the fact that Jesus Christ had his kindness taken for weakness he got crucified. Throughout the gospels people can see that Satan was trying to kill Jesus Christ even before his birth by trying to kill Mary, his mother, who was a virgin, who got pregnant with Jesus, through the Holy Spirit. The people would have believed Mary cheated on Joseph and stoned her to death if God did not come go Joseph in a dream to tell him to get out of their village with Mary. Satan finally convinced the people to crucify Jesus Christ, but it only happened because it was finished. God's will had been done and Jesus won for all of humankind.

The best part is that Jesus Christ died to forgive sins, but then he arose on the third day to be alive within each and every human. So, what that means is that Satan's plans backfired on him and what Satan did to Christ only gave humankind the chance to be saved from the pits of hell.

Humans must remember that Satan's powers are much stronger than any human and that is why when a human tries to stand against Satan, with their own strength, they will lose every time. Because Satan has set up strongholds throughout every human's life to irritate them and push them to the point of reaction on whatever it is that is getting under their skin. But when living in Christ,

Jesus is the strength in that person and Satan's power stands no chance against Jesus Christ. That has been proven over and over again throughout history.

Satan tricks humans into doing things his way just to cause them punishment in the long run. It is as if Satan is trying to give his punishment to others. Most humans have heard the saying 'Misery loves company'. Well, that's why Satan wants to bring as many humans as he can with him for all eternity to his final destination, which is hell so that he is not the only one that is miserable.

Matthew 12: 22 – 30 says:

> Then was brought unto him one possessed with a devil, blind, and dumb: and he healed him, in so much that the blind and dumb both spake and saw. And all the people were amazed and said, 'is not this the son of David?' But when the Pharisees heard it, they said, 'this fellow doth not cast out devils, but by Beelzebub the prince of the devil. And Jesus knew their thoughts, and said unto them, 'Every kingdom divided against itself is brought to desolation; and every city or house divided against itself shall not stand: and if Satan cast out Satan, he is divided against himself; how shall then his kingdom stand? And if I by Beelzebub cast out devils, by whom do your children cast out? Therefore, they shall be your judges. But if I cast out devils by the Spirit of God, then the kingdom of God is come unto you. Or else how can one enter into a strong man's house and spoil his house. He that Is not with me is against me; and he that gathereth not with me scattereth abroad.'

Chapter 7

The Temptations Humans Face

Matthew 4: 1 – 11 says:

> Then was Jesus led up of the Spirit into the wilderness
> to be tempted of the devil.
> And when he had fasted forty days and forty nights, he
> was afterward hungered.
> And when the tempter came to him, he said, 'if thou be
> the Son of God, command that these stones be made bread.'
> But he answered and said, 'it is written man shall not live
> by bread alone, but by every word that proceedeth out
> of the mouth of God.'
> Then the devil taketh him up into the holy city, and setteth him
> on a pinnacle of the temple, and saith unto him, 'if thou be the
> Son of God, cast thyself down: for it is written he shall give
> his angels charge concerning thee: and in their hands they
> shall bear thee up, last at any time thou dash thy foot
> against a stone.'
> Jesus said unto him, 'it is written again, thou shalt not tempt
> the Lord thy God.'
> Again, the devil taketh him up into an exceeding high
> mountain, and sheweth him all the kingdoms of the world,
> and the glory of them; and saith unto him, 'all these things
> will I give thee if thou wilt fall down and worship m.'
> Then saith Jesus unto him 'Get thee hence, Satan: for it is written,
> thou shalt worship the Lord thy God, and him only shalt
> thou serve.'
> Then the devil leaveth him, and, behold angels came and
> ministered unto him.

The enemy tempts humans with the lust of the eye, the lust of the flesh, and with the pride of life, but people must know that the enemy can only tempt them with something that they want. That is simply because a human cannot be tempted with something they do not want.

When humans are tempted the temptations come from the enemy, but God always turns the enemy's temptation into a test to see where the human's faith is. In the word of God, Eve was tempted to eat the fruit by the serpent who was her enemy. The enemy tempted her with the lust of her eyes, flesh and the pride of life. Her eyes cause her to see that the tree was good for food. The pride of life caused her to want to be wise, and her flesh caused her to grab the fruit the tree, then eat.

Well, the enemy never changed, and he tries to use the same temptations on humankind today as he did back then when he did it to Adam and Eve. When humans are not walking in Jesus Christ they fall into temptation every time because of the fact that humans only see what they want instead of what they are created for.

Humans all have temptations, but they do not all have the same temptations. Some humans may be tempted by drugs, by having sex with random people, by fighting with others by being argumentative, by pointing out someone else's flaws, gambling, stealing, on and on. Whatever a human's temptation is, the enemy knows what to do to get that person to fall into their temptation – even when that person is trying not to.

If humans would only trust in God enough to allow Jesus Christ to change the desired of their hearts, then the enemy will no longer be able to get them caught up in falling victim to the temptations that the enemy is constantly trying to bait them into. When a human does fall, through faith in God, grace and the blood of Jesus Christ will wash away their sins.

Struggles

Matthew 5: 3 – 12 says:

> Blessed are the poor in Spirit: for theirs is the Kingdom of Heaven. Blessed are they that mourn for they shall be comforted.
> Blessed are the meak: for they shall inherit the earth.
> Blessed are they which do hunger and thirst after righteousness: for they shall be filled.
> Blessed are the merciful: for they shall obtain mercy.
> Blessed are the peacemakers: for they shall be called children of God.
> Blessed are they which are persecuted for righteousness' sake: for theirs is the Kingdom of Heaven.
> Blessed are ye when men shall revils you, and persecute you, and shall say all manner of evil against you falsely, for my sake.
> Rejoice, and be exceeding glad: for great is your reward in heaven: for so persecuted they the prophets which were before you.

Struggles can be used by the enemy to try making a human fall into temptation. The enemy will cause struggle in a person's life just to make them give up on Christ. And without Christ, humans get tricked by the enemy every time.

The enemy can and will do all that he can as long as humans give him the chance to. He will cause strife in a marriage, he will cause humans to fall behind on bills, he can cause a child to be disobedient to their parents, he can cause a person's car to break down. The enemy has so many tricks and he know exactly how to use them to get person's attention on the world and off of God's will.

No one likes to struggle, but when humans give their struggles to God and allow Christ to deal with them, it causes growth in their life. Humans will begin to gain perseverance, character and hope. That is why it is so important to stand in Christ through everything, whether it's good or bad, hard or easy, because no matter what it is, through Christ it will always work out for the good.

Struggles can cause humans to turn away from God's will and back to what they think they know, which are worldly ways, just to get by in life. Humans may do things like use others to benefit themselves. Men may use women to take care of them while they lay around and do nothing. Then on the other hand a woman may use a man to make sure they are taken care of, even when their heart is not in it. Humans may deal drugs, seek people stolen goods or maybe even buy stolen goods just to get a better price.

Humans do those things to avoid the struggle and those things are truly not worth doing just to have a little pocket money. Humans must remember that Jesus Christ paid the price so that he can deal with all struggles that may come along, for anybody. Humans should always give their struggles to Christ so that God can use them in a righteous way.

The enemy does not care what temptations he needs to use to remove a person's eyes off of Christ he will even take someone's life. A lot of times the enemy tried to get humans to blame themselves or even God for someone's death who was close. By doing that humans tend to do wrong while blaming what they are doing on the death of the person they were close to. In the end, they are only giving the enemy a foothold on their life and he begins to pull them into his evil ways through all of the temptations he tempts them with.

When humans fall into the temptations of the enemy, they begin to move further and further away from Jesus Christ. Then humans tend to start thinking that the wrong that they are doing is right. They also begin to think that they are better than the next person, simply because they are in a better position in life.

Humans all get to where they are in life because of God, but the enemy is so tricky that he can cause humans to think that everything they have in life is no good, so they're not thankful for it, and because of that a human can lose everything. The enemy is the tempter of all tempters, he is very clever, and he will con a con man. But Jesus Christ has him under his feet and as long as people are living in Christ the enemy is under their feet as well.

When following Jesus Christ humans must keep their eyes on the prize and on Jesus Christ for dear life. It is very important that humans see the enemy when he is tempting them so that they can give it to Christ and receive the victory over the enemy. While humans are walking in Jesus Christ they still trip and fall over the temptations that the enemy tempts them with every single time if they do not see what the enemy is doing beforehand. This is because a person will always trip and fall into the ditch if they are looking behind and cannot see what is in front of them. Humans can glance to the side for one second and can find themselves in a ditch that they cannot see themselves climbing out of.

The best thing about Jesus Christ is that, when humans do mess up and fall into the ditch, he is always there to get them out, as long as they ask. But remember the tempter is there, trying to tempt humans who are in Jesus Christ every step of the way.

The battle Is Within

Humans have an ongoing war within them, every second of every day. That war is spiritual. For humans do not war against flesh and blood, but against principalities, powers of rulers of darkness and spiritual wickedness. Humans who are of the world do not understand that this battle is real, but the followers of Jesus Christ do, because they have faith that God sent them the word to help them understand what they are up against.

There is no way that humans can win this battle without Jesus Christ, no matter how good they do or how nice they are. Humans will always get pushed around in circles if they are not living with Christ. This war is going on, within everybody, because not only did Satan get cast down from heaven, but all those who followed him did as well, and Satan is hard at work every second of every day because he knows that his time is short.

If humans do not see this battle that is going on within them, then how will they ever seek to find a way to win? Humans must pray that God opens their spiritual eyes, so that they are no longer blind to the spiritual war that is within them, once humans see what's going on they will then begin to understand that they are helpless and too weak to overcome this battle without Jesus Christ.

Jesus Has Won

Jesus Christ has already won this spiritual battle for humankind and when humans are living in Christ, Christ is living in them, therefore they have victory. Every morning that a believer wakes up they must put on the armor of God, which is the helmet of salvation, the breastplate of righteousness, the sword of the spirit, which is the word of God, the shield of faith, the belt of truth, plus walking in the gospel and peace. When humans walk in the armor of God, Jesus Christ is in control of the fight since he has already won and the humans who are in Christ are being blessed because the word of God says so.

God says love your enemies and they will be at peace with you. That does not make much sense to humankind, but what god's word says is truth. If humans are not loving their enemies, then they are only trying to fight the battle on their own, which means that they are not truly trusting in God's will.

Humans must remember that God knows and is in control of the battle that believers have going on within them. He knows that humans cannot win and that's why God gave his only begotten son, Jesus Christ to do it for everybody. When humans are trying to do it on their own, they are not allowing Jesus Christ to do what he has already done for humankind. And in doing so, humans are not walking with Jesus Christ, they are only being a slave to the enemy.

There is nothing humankind can possibly do to stop the battle that Is going on within them, but if they are truly walking in Jesus Christ, they will have the victory. Besides, when humans are trying to fight the battle on their own, they are only being prideful and pride is what causes the enemy, Satan, the tempter of all to fall in the first place.

Ephesians 6: 10 – 20 says:

Finally, my brethren, be strong in the Lord, and in the
power of his might.
Put on the whole armor of God, that ye may be able
to stand against the wiles of the devil.
For we wrestle not against flesh and blood, but against
principalities, against powers, against the rulers of the
darkness of this word, against spiritual
wickedness in high places.
Wherefore take unto you the whole armor of God,
that ye may be able to withstand in the evil day,
and having done all, to stand.
Stand therefore, having your loins girt about with truth,
and having on the breastplate of righteousness; and
your feet shod with the preparation of the gospel of
peace; above all, taking the shield of faith, wherewith we
shall be able to quench all the fiery darts of the wicked.
And take the helmet of salvation, and the sword of the
spirit, which is the word of God: Praying always with all prayer
and supplication in the Spirit, and watching there unto
with all perseverance and supplication for all saints;
and for me, that utterance may be given unto me,
that I may open my mouth boldly, to make known the
mystery of the gospel, for which I am an ambassador in
bonds: that therein I may speak boldly, as I ought to speak.

Chapter 8

The Love of Jesus Christ

1 Corinthians 13: 1 – 8, 13 says:

> Though I speak with the tongues of men and of angels,
> and have not love, I am become as sounding Brass,
> or a tinkling cymbal.
> And though I have the gift of prophecy, and understand
> all mysteries, and all knowledge; and though I have
> all faith, so that I could remove mountains, and have
> not love, I am nothing.
> Love suffereth long, and is kind; love envieth not;
> love vaunteth not itself, is not puffed up, doth not
> behave itself unseemly, seeketh not her own,
> is not easily provoked, thinketh no evil; beareth all
> things, believeth all things endureth al things.
> Love never faileth: but whether there be prophecies,
> they shall fail; whether there be tongues,
> they shall cease, whether there be knowledge,
> it shall vanish away.
> And now abideth faith, hope, love, these three,
> but the greatest of these is love.

I am sure that by now the fact that God is love has been made clear. Jesus Christ is one with God, which is why he takes on the same characteristic and that's why Jesus is the perfect example of love.

Many people say they love each other. But the question is this: do they truly have the love of Jesus Christ dwelling within their hearts or are they professing a worldly love? The only way a human can truly love is by allowing

Jesus Christ to love through them, because when humans do not allow Christ to love through them, they tend to love the way they have loved from the beginning of times. That kind of love is off and on because humans love only when they are being loved back.

Jesus Christ continued to love even when humankind put him on the cross, drove nails through his hands, feet, the they laughed and mocked him about being the Son of God. Jesus Christ want to the cross to show humankind how much God truly loves them. The love of Jesus Christ will never change no matter what humans do wrong or right because his heart is pure, and Jesus will always want what is best for humankind.

And God loves humans to the point that he gave his only begotten son as a living sacrifice to give humans another way to be a part of his kingdom, for all eternity. Just sit back and think for one second of having one son who by the way was perfect. Now ask yourself this, would you allow your son to give his life for those who killed him?

Everything that God sent his Son here to this earth to do was impossible for humankind to do on their own. No matter how hard they tried humans could not do it. Nowadays humans following Jesus Christ is the only way they can experience the life that he has created them to live. The love of Jesus Christ is very important for a believer to have, while walking with him.

Humans love God because he first loved them but if humans cannot love one another then there is no way they can love God who they cannot see. When humans love God, they look at the fact that he loves everyone and that's why Jesus died. He died to forgive everyone's sins. The only way that humans can truly love God back is by giving their life to him and allowing Jesus Christ to love the Father through them. Since Jesus Christ is the only way to God and he died then rose again, living though him is the only way to love God.

The fact of the matter is that when Jesus Christ is living through a person, he is loving everyone, even that person's enemies because Jesus died to forgive their sins as well. If humans hate someone for what they did to them, they are not loving God and the love of Jesus Christ is not within them. There is always going to be people, who will do a person wrong, even when that person is loving them because no one is perfect.

The word of God lets humans know that if the world first hated Jesus Christ then who are the followers of Jesus Christ not to be hated. Just because someone hates a person does not mean that God will not keep peace within the hater's heart, even if he hates a person who is doing God's will. This is said because the word of God also lets humans know that If they love their enemies, then their enemies will be at peace with them. This peace with the enemy thing that God speaks of does not make much sense to humans but stepping out on faith is the only thing that is going to prove God's word to be truth.

Ephesians 5: 1,2 says, " Be ye therefore followers of God, as dear children; and walk in love, as Christ also hath loved us, and hath given himself for us an offering and a sacrifice to God for a sweet smelling savor."

The Importance of Love

The word of God lets humans know that they should abide in faith, hope, and love. But then the word of God goes on to say, the greatest of those three things is love. When humans look at the life of Jesus Christ, they can see that Jesus Christ is faith, hope and love, when a person is walking in Christ, they are abiding in faith, hope, love and much more. Love can be painful at times, but it is always worthwhile. If God himself was not love, then he would not have sent his only begotten Son to save humankind, and that is the example of true love.

When reading the word of God, the love of God is shown all throughout scriptures, even in the Old Testament. For a perfect example, look to the Book of Ruth. It was the love of God in her that caused her to stay with her mother in law, even when things did not look good at ll. Humans can see the love of God in the 10 commandments that God gave to Moses. When looking deeper than just a list of rules, they will see that when they break those rules, they are only hurting themselves as well as others. However, if they follow God's will, they will avoid going through a whole lot of pain in their life.

John, the son of Zebedee and brother of James, had a true love for the Lord and in the letters, he wrote he speaks of loving God by allowing the light of Jesus Christ to shine. He speaks of all things being made for Jesus Christ. He speaks of God loving the world and about humans loving one another. John truly loved and spent time with Jesus Christ while he was here on this earth.

Elizabeth, who was John's mother, was related to Mary the mother of Jesus Christ. Jesus Christ had a love for John, before John even knew of him. When

Mary met with Elizabeth while they were pregnant, John jumped for joy in Elizabeth's womb because he became filled with the Holy Spirit and that's when his love for Jesus Christ began.

The Way Humans Love God

The only way humans can truly love God is by allowing his will to be done their life. When humans are following Jesus Christ, they are allowing God's will to be done, they must be dying to themselves daily and allowing Christ to live through them. Then they become a temple for the living God. They deny what they want, they pick up their cross and follow Jesus Christ.

A human's cross can be anything that they may be going through in life, good or bad, whatever it is they must give it to God for Jesus Christ to use. Loving God is a person giving him, their thoughts, their plans, their words, their faith, their love, their hope, their friendships, their family and most importantly their life to God as a living sacrifice for Christ to live, trusting that he knows exactly what to do with those things. It may seem as if humans have worked so hard to receive the things that they have in life, but at the end of the day humans can have all they want and it will not profit them any if they do not have love.

When humans are not loving God, they do not know how to truly love themselves or anybody else.

1 John 4: 7 – 15 says:

Beloved, let us love one another: for love is God; and
everyone that is born of god, and knoweth god.
He that loveth not knoweth not God; for God is love.

In this was manifested the love of God toward us because
  God sent his only begotten Son into the world,
  that we might live through him.
Herein Is love, not that we loved God, but that he loved us,
  and sent his Son to be the propitiation for our sins.
Beloved, if God so loved us, we ought also to love one another.
No man hath seen God at any time.
If we love one another, God dwelleth in us, and his
  love is perfect in us.
Hereby know we that we dwell in him and he in us,
  because he hath given us of his spirit.
And we have seen and do testify that the Father sent the
  Son to be the savior of the world.
Whosoever shall confess that Jesus is the Son of God.
God dwelleth in him, and he in God.

The Gospel in One Word Is Love

The word of God tells humans to love their neighbor as their brother. Jesus Christ preached love with his words and actions. The word of God also lets people know what happens when they do not love and when they do not love they are only hating others in their heart. With hatred in a human's heart they can become liars, thieves, murderers, fornicators, and more. Humans will also have no guilty conscience for doing those things.

In the word of God Cain killed Abel, his own brother because he was not truly loving God. All the other deaths that happen in the word of God were simply because of the fact that humans were not loving God. A lot of times in the word, those who truly loved God died, because of the works of those who were not loving God. It sounds bad, but it's not, because the word of God states that to live is Christ and to die is gain

When truly having faith In God, humans love him enough to believe everything in his word. No one wants to die but in Christ people know that they live forever and that the life here on this earth is only temporary. This life is only a building block for the relationship with Christ to strengthen the hope, faith and most importantly love of God that is within humankind.

The more humans surrender, the more they love and the more they love, the more they see how true that word of God is. Through the love of God, humans are made conquerors and when they truly love God, they will conquer everything they may go through in life. Humans must first ask in prayer for the love of Jesus Christ to be in their heart, and God will give them that love. It will not happen overnight, but it will happen, because the word of God says ask in the name of Jesus and you will receive. So, let's do what the gospel says by surrendering any hate that is being held onto in the heart and let's love one another.

1 John 4: 16 – 21 says:

> And we have known and believed the love that
>   God hath for us.
> God is love; and he that dwelleth in love dwelleth in God,
>   and God in him.
> Herein is our love made perfect, that we may have boldness
>   in the day of judgement: because as he is,
>   so are we in this world.
> There is not fear in love; but perfect love casteth out fear:

because fear hath torment.

He that feareth is not made perfect in love.

We love him because he first loved us.

If a man says, I love God, and hateth his brother, he is a liar:

for he, that loveth not his brother whom he hath seen,

how can he love God whom he hath not seen?

And this commandment have we from him, that he

who loveth God love his brother also.

Chapter 9

The Lord wants to Give His Riches

Ephesians 1: 2 – 10 says:

> Grace be to you, and peace, from God our Father,
>   and from the Lord Jesus Christ.
> Blessed be the God and Father of our Lord Jesus Christ,
>   who hath blessed us with all spiritual blessings in
>   heavenly places in Christ: According as he hath chosen
>   us in him before the foundation of the world,
>   that we should be holy and without blame before
>   him in love: having predestinated us unto the adoption
>   of children by Jesus Christ to himself, according to the Good
>   pleasure of his will, to the praise of the glory of his grace,
>   wherein he hath made us accepted in the beloved.
> In whom we have redemption through his bold, the forgiveness
>   of sins, according to his good pleasure which he hath
>   proposed in himself: that in the dispensation of the
>   fullness of times he might gather in one all things in
>   Christ, both which are in heaven, and which are on
>   earth; even in him.

Jesus Christ wants to fill humans with his richness, he wants to use everything that humankind has been through to bring glory to the Father. To receive the riches that are in store for humankind, humans must chase after Christ and not after what the world has to offer. When humans seek God with everything they do, God promises that he will make them rich. God is not speaking of having a lot of money, because that is worldly. The most important riches are stored in heaven.

The word of God says that the love of money is the root of evil. The word of God also asks what it profits to gain the world and lose your soul. Well, when doing God's will by following Jesus Christ, God will give humans their heart's desires and who in the world can honestly say that they do not want to be rich.

When humans become mature enough in Christ to receive what they have been called in life to do, then God will give it to them. In fact, when humans ask God for something in the mighty name of Jesus Christ God will and does give them their blessing. But the thing is , when humans are not mature enough in Jesus Christ to allow him to use whatever it is that God blessed them with to glorify God's name, they do not truly know how to use the blessings that God gave them. Therefore, their blessings are being stripped away by the enemy himself.

Just ask yourself these questions when God allows a human to have a lot of money here on earth: What do they do with it and why? Would they use the money to glorify the Father's name? if so, how? Or would they use the money to glorify their own name? These are some of the question's humans should ask themselves when being blessed enough to have a wealth here on earth. When humans use their blessings to glorify God's name, it is impossible for the enemy to use their blessings in the wrong way.

The riches of the Lord allow humans to live richly, spiritually, physically, and mentally. Most people think of having success in a high paying job as riches, but without the riches of the Lord, humans will always feel empty on the inside. Humans can have everything they want here on this earth, but yet still feel empty on the inside. Without Jesus Christ they will always feel empty. Yes, it has been said, the riches of the Lord are found in Jesus Christ and what Christ has can be anybody's as long as they accept the gift of God's grace, which is Jesus Christ in their heart.

God wants every human to receive his gift of grace so that they will no longer be like lost sheep in this world without their shepherd. Even if humans have nothing of the world, but have the riches of the Lord, they will never feel empty. They will know through faith in Jesus Christ, the Son of God who lives within all, what is manifesting within their lives.

Matthew 13: 18 – 23 says:

> Hear ye therefore the parable of the shower.
> When anyone heareth the word of the Kingdom,
>   and understandeth it not, then cometh the wicked one,
>   and catcheth away that which was sown in his heart.
> This is he that received seed by the wayside.
> But he who received the seed into stony places,
>   the same is he that heareth the word, and anon with
>   Joy receiveth it; yet hath he not root in himself, but
>   dureth for awhile: for when tribulation or persecution ariseth,
>   because of the word, by and by he is offended.
> He also that received seed among the thorns is he that
>   heareth the word; and the care of this world,
>   and the deceitfulness of riches, choke the word,
>   and he becometh unfruitful.
> But he that received seed into the good ground is he that
>   heareth the word, and understandeth it; which also
>   beareth fruit, and bringeth forth, some an hundredfold,
>   some sixty, some thirty.

Living in God's Grace

Romans 5: 1 – 6 says:

> Therefore, being justified by faith, we have peace with
> God through our Lord Jesus Christ: By whom also we have
> access by faith into this grace wherein we stand and
> rejoice in hope of the glory of God.
> And not only so, but we glory in tribulations also:
> knowing that tribulation worketh patience; and patience,
> experience; and experience, hope: and hope maketh not
> ashamed; because the love of God is shed abroad in our
> hearts by the Holy Ghost which is given unto us.
> For when we were yet without strength, in due time
> Christ died for the ungodly.

To live in God's grace, humans must first believe and accept Jesus Christ in their heart. There is nothing any human can do, good or bad to determine if they will receive god's gift of grace because God's grace is a gift to al who are strong enough to accept it. Without God's gift of grace in a human's life they do nothing except living life dead in sin. But through God's undying grace humankind can be saved.

Humans all can receive grace through faith and faith comes by hearing the word of God. So, if humans do not continually hear or read the word of God, they will not know what to have faith in. Without faith in the Son of God, it is impossible to have grace.

When living in God's grace humans begin to sin less because through faith, they begin to become aware of how bad their sins are hurting themselves and because they are hurting themselves, they are hurting God. On top of that when humans do sin, they begin to seek forgiveness. While seeking forgiveness they then turn to God and away from their sinful nature, which in God's word means they are repenting from their sins.

Through faith humans believe that they are always wrong, but yet they know that they are forgiven. That way they can forgive themselves as well as other when they do something horribly wrong. At the same time, they know that the sins have been washed away, because of God's gift of grace.

Humans can see God's grace in any and everything they go through. It does not matter if they think it is good or bad, God's grace is there, and humans will always find God's grace as long as they seek to receive it. To see God's grace humans, need to pray, and most importantly surrender how they are feeling along with what they want to do over to God. This is so they can be calm enough to hear his still small voice.

The more and more humans step off into God's grace the better off they are, because they are another step closer to God. When humans think they are doing everything right, that is when they are wrong because they are no longer standing in God's grace. In fact, they are walking further and further away from God.

No matter how good humans are doing or think they are doing in life, there is always going to be pain one way or the other. There is always going to be something happening in a person's life that the person will have no understanding of. But through the grace of God humans can receive understanding of anything and everything that happens in life.

Most preachers do not preach much about God' grace. It tends to make people think that they can just do whatever they want without repenting and yet still be forgiven. However, if a person is truly standing in God's, it will cause a total change in that person's heart, which is why God's grace means everything and without God's grace humans are reduced to nothing more than what they are born into: sin.

Genesis 1: 26 – 30 says:

And God said; let us make men in our image, after our likeness: and let them have dominion over the fish of the sea, and over the fowl of the air, and over the cattle, and over all the earth, and over every creeping thing that creepeth upon the earth. So God created man in his own image, in the image of God created he him; male and female created he them. And God blessed them, and God said unto them, be fruitful and multiply, and have dominion over the fish of the sea, and over the fowl of the air, and over every living thing that moveth upon the earth. And God said, behold, I have given you every herb bearing seed, which is upon the face of the earth, and every tree, in which is the fruit of a tree yielding seed; to you it shall be for meat. And to every beast of the earth, and to every fowl of the air, and to everything that creepeth upon the earth, wherein there is life, I have given every green herd for meat: and it was so.

Chapter 10

Running the Race with Jesus Christ

Hebrews 12: 1 – 6 says:

> Wherefore seeing we also are compassed about with
> so great a cloud of witnesses, let us lay aside every weight,
> and the sin which doth so easily beset us, and let us run
> with patience the race that is set before us, looking unto
> Jesus the author and finisher of our faith; who for the Joy
> that was set before him endured the cross, despising the
> shame and is set down at the right and of the throne of God.
> For consider him that endured such contradiction of sinners
> against himself, lest ye be wearied and faint in your minds.
> Ye have not yet resisted unto blood, striving against sin.
> And ye have forgotten the exhortation which speaketh
> unto you as unto children, my son, despise not thou the
> chastening of the Lord, nor faint when thou art rebuked of him:
> For whom the Lord loveth the chasteneth, and scourgeth every
> son whom he receiveth.

When running this race of life, humans must run with Jesus Christ. Why? Because Jesus Christ is everything. Jesus Christ is everywhere at once. He hears everything that is going on and he is the reason for everything that was created.

When running this race humans must run with a speed that is not going to gas them out. Some people may run faster than others. Some people may speed walk. Some people may even need to crawl. It doesn't matter, because as long as they are moving forward, they are making progress.

Humans can sometimes make a mistake by turning around and falling in to the past or even into their past ways. What humans should always remember is that God is a forgiving God. Not only does God forgive, but he forgets as well. That means as long as humans keep their eyes on Jesus Christ while running in the race their past will no longer matter anymore. In fact, a human's past will only be used as a boost to get to the finish line.

While running this race there will be many obstacles that will cause a human to stumble, maybe even fall off of the track. The word of God lets humans know that the pathway is straight, narrow and that the pathway is Jesus Christ. This lifelong race is impossible to participate in without depending on the strength of Jesus Christ to carry humans through.

The further humans go in this race the more it causes them to grow. Humans begin to grow more and more in Jesus Christ. They begin to walk like Christ talk like Christ, think like Christ and most importantly love like Christ.

There is no shortcut, but the pathway is lit up. There is danger along the way, but humans have all the protection they need. There will be storms from time to time along the way, but humans will always have shelter. As long as they put God first along the way, they will never backtrack.

Sometimes other humans move faster than others, but the prize that humans should be focused on is the same no matter what place they come in. In fact, the word of God speaks of the last being first and the first being last. The fact that the first will be last and the last will be first does not make much sense, but God is an awesome God and those who came last will be much stronger than those who came first. Why? Because they would have been through more with Christ than those who came first and as a result, they will be stronger spiritually.

This race is more important than any other race that anyone will run in life and this race will take a lifetime to cross the finish line. It does not matter what place a human finishes, because as long as they finish, they win. When they win, they all win the same prize. So, let's all be strong in Jesus Christ and win the race that humans have been predestined to win.

This has probably been said more than once so far in this book, but it can never be said enough. Just in case it was missed the first or second time: the word of God lets humans know that sorrow is better for the heart than laughter. That's because when humans have what they want, they do not seek to find what it is they want, and the word of God lets humans know if they seek they will find. God's wisdom brings humans to this understanding: when humans go through pain while seeking God's will, their spiritual being begins to grow through overcoming the hurt.

It's like when a human works out to better their outer appearance. It hurts which causes the flesh to go through the healing process. But when that happens the body looks better, feels better, and gets stronger. Humans must keep working out through the pain, when doing so the results continue to get better. When a person first starts working out it hurts much more than when they had been doing it for a while. On the other hand, the results come much faster with less work when a human first starts working out. A person must break down to a point where the flesh can understand what the word says.

Most of the time humans tend to strive for the outer, fleshly appearance to get better. If they really put thought into it their outer appearance is only a temporarily shell for their inner, which is spiritual. Not that working out the physical is not a good thing, it's just that the inner, which is the spirit and soul, is what lives on when the flesh dies off no matter what is done.

Psalm 19: 5 – 9 says, "Which is as a bridegroom coming out of his chamber, and rejoiceth as a strong man to run a race. His going forth is from the end of heaven, and his circuit unto the ends of it: and there is nothing hid from the heart thereof."

Chapter 11

The Lord's Timing is Perfect

Matthew 21: 21 – 22 says:

> Jesus answered and said unto them, 'verily I say unto you,
>> if ye have faith, and doubt not, ye shall say not only do
>> this which is done to the fig tree, but also if ye shall say
>> unto this mountain, be thou removed, and be thou cast
>> into the sea; it shall be done.
> And all thing whatsoever ye shall ask In prayer,
>> believing, ye shall receive.'

Humans seem to pray all the time for their wants and needs, but then they expect their prayers to be answered overnight. Well, that is not the way that God's will works. God knows that a human being blessed can also be a curse, if the blessings are used in the wrong manner.

This is one of the reasons why God allows humans to go through tribulation, hoping that they will lean on his word to overcome. God knows that when humans depend on him and his ways, their faith begins to grow, which causes them to depend on him more and more through times of need. When depending on God humans grow stronger and they are also being built so that they are able to handle the blessings that God wants them to receive.

It is a must that humans take the time to allow God to answer their prayers in a righteous manner, without giving up on him before he answers. The reason for that is because the Lord knows exactly what humans need and if they give up on trusting in him, they might receive the blessings and then turn around and use them in a wrong way.

The longer humans wait and the harder it gets on them, the bigger the blessings will be. That's why humans must hang on to God's word through everything, even when it seems as if nothing is going to work out. When it feels as if it won't work out, God himself has the door wide open. If a human step through that door with faith, then they will step right into the Lord's blessings. But when a human gives up it's as if they turn away from the door and they begin to walk further away from God and the blessings, which God has for them.

Some people may laugh or mock a person because of their faith, but that should never be enough to cause a person to give up if they are truly following Christ. One of the main reasons why humans should never give up, when others are laughing or mocking their faith is because the people of the world first laughed and mocked Jesus Christ. If it wasn't for what he did, humans wouldn't have a way to God and his Kingdom.

That is because Jesus Christ is the one who was hung on the cross for the forgiveness of sin. He is the one who every knee will bow to. Jesus is the one that every single tongue will confess to being Lord forever.

Sometimes Humans Make Their Waiting Time Harder

When humans start falling away from Christ, by not reading the word, or by not giving everything to Jesus Christ, humans make things harder on themselves. Without the help of Jesus Christ, they only begin to bear everything upon their own shoulders instead of allowing Jesus to carry whatever it is that they are trying to handle on their own. Humans should not be worried about anything and at the same time they should be thanking God for everything.

Humans make waiting on the Lord hard when they are trying to do things on their own, because when doing things on their own they fail to understand that they really have no control of the outcome. No matter what a human does to try and change the outcome of something, it always seems to come out wrong unless they depend on God to make it right. Humans can even sometimes veer off the path and get lost. Because of that they make things harder on themselves. The end result will always work out for good as long as they stand in God's grace.

Humans all wait on the Lord one way or the other. It does not matter if they are with Jesus or against him, but receiving his blessings is another story. When humans just surrender their own will by allowing God's will to be done in their life, Jesus Christ will lead them to the right place, at the right time, so that they can receive the blessings that god is trying to give them.

While waiting humans will face a lot of things that Jesus Christ has already overcome for them. So when they give whatever it is that they are facing to Jesus Christ, He already knows what to do to overcome the situation again. By doing so Jesus Christ will use that person to make a change for his good in the dark world.

Humans are all far from perfect, but the only thing God asks them to do is sit still in His will while the Holy Spirit, Jesus Christ and he himself does all the work. Sometimes humans must wait days, weeks, months, and maybe even years to enjoy the blessings that God gives to them. It can even take a lifetime to truly enjoy God's blessings the way that God meant for them to be enjoyed, but God's promise is sure and all the generations to come will enjoy the blessing that were received by a person who had faith and waited patiently on God's will to be done.

When humans do not sit still and wait for the Lord, they are not looking at the big picture and that picture is the plan that God has for each and every person's life. In that plan God promises to give humans everything he has and God owns everything, because he is the creator of everything. When waiting on his timing God will reveal what he wants for a person, before they even receive it. When they do receive it their faith in the Lord grows.

Humans must wait on the Lord as if they are waiting in a line to get to where they are going.

A woman should wait for God to bring the right man to them, and, on the other hand, men should wait for God to bring the right women by their side. That way their companionship will be strong enough to make it through everything that they may go through as a couple with the Lord. Sometimes humans must wait for God to bring forth the right job, the right contract, the right business partner, the right friend, the right car and anything else a human can possibly thing of, because when it comes from God a human is more thankful for it in the end.

Waiting on the Lord's timing through everything is very pleasing to God because it shows that a human truly trusts in the Lord and his ways with all of their heart. Plus it goes to show that they have faith in what God reveals to them even when nobody else did. The more humans trust in the Lord's ways the more God reveals to them and the more God reveals to them the more God's blessings will flow so that they can receive them.

The word of God states that all humans fall short of God's glory. Because of that, humans tend to jump the gun on waiting for God's will to be done and when doing so it only makes waiting on God to move seem harder than it really is. Humans must do their job by running the race for God by sitting still waiting patiently for his timing so that God's blessings will flow nonstop and not only flow nonstop but be worthwhile when received.

Matthew 6: 9 – 13 says:

> After this manner therefore pray ye: our father which
>
> art in heaven, hallowed by thy name.
>
> Thy kingdom come, they will be done in earth, as it is in heaven.
>
> Give us this day our daily bread, and forgive us our debts,
>
> as we forgive our debtors.
>
> And lead us not into temptation but deliver us from evil:
>
> for thine is the kingdom, and the power,
>
> and the glory, forever. Amen.

Short Testimony

Being in the world lost, I never thought to find a wife. How could I be so blind that I could not see the true blessings God had in store for me? God has already found the women who he took from my lower rib, before I was even thought of.

My mind and heart thought that I was God's gift to women. I could protect them, I could do the hard work around the house, and I could help them relieve their stress through good sex. I was about money. I was fair, I was in good shape. I was good with kids. I was honest. What more could a woman possibly want?

To be honest my mind still thinks the same way, but there is something much different within my heart. That something is my Lord and savior Jesus Christ and his words. Because of that I know the truth and the truth is that God knows who my virtuous woman is. I pray that the eyes of my heart are opened to see her when she comes along, so that I do not deny her.

Chapter 12

When Finding a Spouse

Ephesians 5: 21 – 33 says:

Submitting yourselves one to another in the fear of God.

Wives, submit yourselves to your own husbands,

as unto the lord.

For the husband is the head of the wife, even as Christ

is the head of the church: and he is the savior of the body.

Therefore as the church is subject unto Christ, so let the wives

be to their own husbands in everything.

Husbands, lover your wives, even as Christ also loved the church,

and gave himself for it; that he might sanctify and cleanse

it with the washing of water by the word, that he might

present it to himself a glorious church, not having spot or wrinkle,

or any such thing; but that it should be holy and

without blemish.

So ought men to love their wives as their own bodies.

He that loveth his wife loveth himself.

For no man ever yet hated his own flesh; but nourisheth

and cherisheth it, even as the Lord of the church.

For we are members of his body, of his flesh, and of his bones.

For this cause shall a man leave his father and mother,

and shall be joined unto his wife, and they two shall be one flesh.

This is a great mystery: but I speak concerning Christ and the church.

Nevertheless let everyone of you in particular so love his

wife even as himself; and the wife see that she reverence her husband.

First and foremost, there can be no same sex marriage that can work out according to God's will. Yes, God is a forgiving God if someone has fallen into a same sex relationship they can and will be forgiven as long as they repent, turn from their ways, and stand in God's grace.

When a human is truly seeking forgiveness, they will forgive themselves for their past sins and when doing so they are turning form their old ways and realizing that they were wrong. The world will continually try pulling a person back into their sins if that person is not standing in God's grace daily and being thankful for everything.

Okay. When finding a spouse the word of God states that the male and female are to be equally yoked with one another in Jesus Christ, when that's the matter, God's love will dwell in that relationship forever and ever.

In 1 Corinthians 13, "The word of God truly expresses the love that God has for humankind and when that love is in a relationship, the man and woman always do what they do while thinking of doing for the other. When doing so, they come together as one person in the body of Christ, which means that whatever they do will always come together and work out when everything is said and done. The love of God is so important and that is because without that love, things are done for the wrong reasons.

There are many couples who are of this world who express a worldly love for one another. There are even couples who have stayed married for over 30 years and the results of those kinds of marriages teat the emotions of the couple, along with their children down constantly. It puts the children of that relationship in a lifestyle full of strongholds set up by the enemy himself and it will be up to the children to trust God along with his way to break the strongholds of the enemy.

The only way a child can and will allow God to overcome the strongholds of the enemy is by denying their emotions and by removing their selves from the relationship of their parents as they grow older. The biggest part for the children is they are honest with God and their selves, making sure that their emotions are removed from their parent's relationship or maybe even relationships before they get into a relationship of their own. When they do get into relationship, they must make sure both partners are on the same page, in Christ. If the children are not strong enough in Christ to break the strongholds of the enemy in their lifetime and they continue to do things the only way that they have learned to do them, then everything the enemy has set up will only get even harder on the next generation.

Okay. In finding a spouse that is equally yoked in Christ a man is to follow the word of God in his everyday life and a woman is to do the same. The word of God speaks of husbands loving their wives as Christ loves the church. Well, Christ loved the church enough to give his life to God's will being done for them. The only way a man can do this for his wife is by allowing Christ to live through him, by doing all he does as if he is doing it for Christ to use. On the other hand the wife must obey the scripture as well as if she is giving herself to God as a living sacrifice, to do as Christ wants her to do.

Nowadays the man and women want to take on the role of the man, without having the fear of God in their hearts. The truth is that God made a man a man for a reason and God mad a woman a woman for a reason. That reason is for the man, woman and also the children to enter into the promise of the Kingdom.

Men, in Proverbs 31: 30, 31 the word of God says, "favor is deceitful, and beauty is vain: but a woman that feareth the Lord, she shall be praised. Give her of her hands; and let her own works praise in the gates." Men, the book of proverbs full of God's wisdom and not only does the Book of Proverbs carry scripture to let you know what kind of woman to give your heart to, but the book of proverbs also lets you know what kind of women not to give your heart to. In the book of proverbs there is many scriptures that a woman can read to find out who a God fearing man is and who a foolish man is, not only in the book of Proverbs, but all throughout the word of God.

Women, in 2 Timothy 3: 1 – 7 says:

> This knows also, that in the last days perilous times shall come.
> For men shall be lovers of their own selves, covetous, boasters,
> proud, blasphemers, disobedient to parents, unthankful,
> unholy, without natural affection, truce breakers, false accusers,
> incontinent, fierce, despisers of those that are good,
> traitors, heady, high-minded, lovers of pleasures more than
> lovers of God; having a form of godliness, but denying the power
> thereof: from such turn away.

For of this sort are they which creep into houses,

and lead captive silly women laden with sins, led away with divers lusts,

ever learning, and never able to come to the knowledge of the truth.

The word of God clearly lets women and men know what to look for in their spouse, not only what to look for, but also what to not look for. If humans truly study and follow the word of God it would keep their hearts from being hurt in many different ways. When a man or woman is in a relationship because they are seeking to have the lust of their flesh, that relationship will fail. Why? Because the couple will tear one another down, trying to accomplish what it is that they want for themselves.

On the other hand when a couple is in a God fearing relationship with one another, following God's word every step of the way, then everything the couple does will be about building each other in Christ through everything they can possibly go through together as one. When following the word the man along with the woman will both continually grow and also reach higher places in life. Not only will a couple grow for each other, but if they have children their children will also grow up in a healthy home that is full of growth. Their children will grow up, find the right spouse and repeat the same that they learned growing up.

This is why doing the will of God is so important for a couple, because it will give God the power to break down strongholds that the enemy has set up within the man and women's lives from the past generations and that the couple may not even know about. The word of God also shows the things the enemy will try to do in a relationship and that's because he has been doing it since the beginning of time.

In Genesis 3 1 – 7 says:

Now the serpent was more subtle then any beast of the field
which the Lord God had made.
And he said unto the woman, 'yea, hath God said, ye shall
not eat of every tree of the garden?
'And the woman said unto the serpent 'we may eat of the trees
of the garden: but of the fruit of the tree which is in the midst
of the garden, God hath said, "ye shall not eat of it, neither shall
ye touch it, last ye die."
'And the serpent said unto the woman, 'ye shall not surely die:
For God doth know that in the day ye eat thereof, then your eyes
shall be opened, and ye shall be as gods, knowing good and evil,
'And when the woman said that the tree was good for food,
and that it was pleasant to the eyes, and a tree to be desired
to make one wise, she took of the fruit thereof, and did eat,
and gave also unto her husband with her; and he did eat.
And the eyes of them both were opened, and they knew that they
were naked; and they sewed fig leaves together and
made themselves aprons.

Chapter 13

Living in the Presence of the Lord

Psalm 16: 5 – 11 says:

The Lord is the portion of mine inheritance and of my cup:

thou maintainest my lot.

The lines are fallen unto me in pleasant places; yea,

I have a godly heritage, I will bless the Lord, who hath given

my counsel: my reins also instruct me in the night seasons.

I have set the Lord always before me; because he is at my right

hand, I shall not be moved.

Therefore my heart is glad, and my glory rejoiceth:

my flesh also shall rest in hope.

The presence of the Lord is such a wonderful feeling. There is no worries, no shame, and everything works out for God's glory. The Lord is always present, but most of the time humans do not seek to realize that truth. The Lord is there with everyone, it does not matter if a person knows God is there or not. All the wrong humans can do while hiding it from others, can never be hidden from God.

What a human can do is confess the wrong that they are aware of to God, through prayer, ask for God's forgiveness, believe that he forgave, and ask for the strength to overcome whatever it was that they were doing wrong. For the wrong's a human can be doing without realizing they are doing it, they can simply confess them through prayer by saying this: God forgive me for sins the I have committed against you without knowing I was doing so. Then ask God to reveal the sins to you in a due time because if God reveals them all at once it may be too much for you to bear. When doing these things humans are living in the presence of the Lord and when doing so their spiritual eyes will become open to how good God really is. Humans will begin understanding that they can only imagine how good God really is.

When truly experiencing the presence of the Lord God almighty, humans will experience warmth that cannot be explained with words. The best way to explain it is that it will take all of human's focus off of the world and keeps it all on God. It is a better feeling than any worldly high a human can experience in the world, and yet living in the presence of God is the best thing for a human to do in life, because with the Lord they will live a long and prosperous life.

When humans are not living in the presence of the Lord they tend to do wrong to others who are trying to do the right things in life. Most of the time, humans tend to cause someone else to stumble and even fall into their childish ways when they are not standing in the presence of the Lord. When humans are not standing in the presence of the Lord, it is not that God is not present; it is that humans turn their backs on God when they're not.

Like it was said before God is present always no matter what, but when humans allow worldly ways to overtake them, it causes their spiritual eyes to be covered with a veil so that they can no longer see or feel the presence of the Lord and what it is that God has really done for humankind. Jesus did not just get on the cross to die for the forgiveness of sin, and then stop there. He rose again so that he can live through each and every human, so that he can continue to do

God's will through them. God put his only begotten Son upon the cross so that his light can be here on this earth, for humankind, because all humans need the light.

At the same time God loves humans enough to give them a free will to do as they want. It's the human's job to love God first, themselves and their families enough to trust in God to give them their heart's desires, in the right way, so that they won't lose them once they receive them. Not only will God transform a human's heart's desires from evil to righteous in his eyes for himself, but for their benefit. This is the very reason why it's so important for humans to surrender their will end to live in the presence of the Lord, God almighty.

Psalm 139: 7 -14 says:

> Wither shall I go from thy spirit? Or wither shall I flee from
>
> thy presence?
>
> If I ascend up into heaven, thou art there: if I make my bed in hell,
>
> behold, thou art there.
>
> If I take the wings of the morning, and dwell in the uttermost part
>
> of the sea; even there shall they hand lead me, and thy right hand
>
> shall hold me, if I say, surely the darkness shall cover me; even the
>
> night shall be light about me.
>
> Yea, the darkness hideth not from thee; but the night shineth as the
>
> day: the darkness and the light are both alike to thee.
>
> For thou hast possessed my reins: thou hast covered me in my
>
> mother's womb.
>
> I will praise thee; for I am fearfully and wonderfully made:
>
> marvellous are thy works; and that my soul knoweth right well.

In the word of God there is a story of a man by the name of Jonah who was fleeing from the presence of the Lord. Although he was fleeing from God, he did not get away, no matter where he went. Eventually a bad enough situation happened in his life that caused those around Jonah to throw Jonah overboard from a ship just to save their own lives.

After Jonah was thrown overboard the storm stopped and the other men who were on the ship were safe. Not only were the men safe but Jonah was as well. When he was thrown overboard a very big fish swallowed him up. Jonah was in the belly of the fish for three days and three nights.

While in the belly of the fish Jonah began to speak with God, not only was Jonah speaking, but the most important part was that Jonah was listening. Because Jonah was in the belly of the fish while in the middle of the sea with no way out, Jonah was in a situation where he could depend on no one else except for God. As soon as Jonah made the promise to do God's will by living in the presence of the Lord, God ordered the fish to spit Jonah up. Not only did the fish spit Jonah up, but the fish had swum from the middle of the sea to spit Jonah up on dry land.

A lot of the time humans are fleeing from the presence of the Lord and they find themselves in situations that they cannot get out of on their own. On top of that, everyone they were around tends to leave them for dead, just like the man on the ship did to Jonah when they threw him overboard and left him in the middle of the sea to drown. Well, if you or someone you know is in a rough situation in life, it's as if you or that person is in the belly of the fish. It's probably, because you or that person is fleeing from the presence of the Lord.

If that is the case just see to it that there is surrender to the will of God. Promise to live in the presence of the Lord. Then sit back with faith as you see that situation that was too much to handle fall apart.

Jonah 2: 1 -10 says:

> Then Jonah prayed unto the Lord his God out of the fish's belly,
> and said, 'I cried by reason of mine affliction unto the Lord, and
> he heard me; out of the belly of hell cried I, and thou heardest
> my voice.
> For thou hadst cast me into the deep, in the midst of the seas
> and the floods compassed over me.
> Then I said, I am cast out of thy sight; yet I will look again toward
> thy holy temple.
> The waters compassed me about, even to the soul: the depth
> closed me round about, the weeds were wrapped about my head.
> I went down to the bottoms of the mountains; the earth with her
> bars was about me forever: yet hast thou brought up my life from
> corruption, o Lord my God.
> When my soul fainted within me I remembered the Lord:
> and my prayer came in unto thee, into thine holy temple.
> They that observe lying vanities forsake their own mercy
> But I will sacrifice unto thee with the voice of thanksgiving;
> I will pray that, that I have vowed.

Salvation if of the Lord.

And the Lord spake unto the fish, and it vomited

out Jonah up on the dry land.

Living with the Fear of God

Ecclesiastes 12: 4 – 7 says:

And the doors shall be shut in the streets, when the sound of

the grinding is low, and he shall rise up at the voice of the bird,

and all the daughters of music shall be brought low;

also when they shall be afraid of that which is high, and fears

shall be in the way, and the almond tree shall flourish,

and the grasshopper shall be a burden, and desire shall fail:

because man goeth to his long home, and the mourners go about

the streets: or ever the silver cord be loosed, or the golden

bowl be broken, or the pitcher be broken at the cistern.

Then shall the dust return to the earth as it was: and the spirit

shall return unto God who gave it.

Most of the time humans live life in fear of death and in what another human can do to them, but with the fear of the Lord, humankind will overcome those fears. The fear of the Lord is so powerful, because it's not about fearing what God will do it's more about fearing him not doing what he does to save human. If humans don't have God they don't even have the very air they breathe. Humans should understand that without Jesus Christ being in their life, they are only facing a death sentence. Humans are like sheep without a shepherd and sheep without a shepherd are dumb enough to walk off the edge of a cliff while eating.

When humans have the fear of the Lord in their heart, they can make the right decisions at the right time. With the fear the Lord humans tend to allow God to save them a lot of pain and trouble, because when choosing God's will, humans no longer go through anything without allowing Christ to go through it for them. Humans must understand that fearing the Lord is a big step in letting Christ grow in their heart.

Living with the fear of the Lord in the heart allows God's purpose the be done through each and everything a human can possibly go through in life, including pain and suffering, because the word of God shows that Jesus Christ uses it all. If Jesus Christ can use everything to glorify the Father, and humans allow him to, then why do humans fear what the world can do? Worldly fears allow the world to stop them from giving everything to God to glorify his name.

What humans fear in the worldly realm Jesus Christ has already overcome. When humans have the fear of the Lord in their heart, they will then understand that there is nothing the world or anybody who is of the world, in that case, can do to them, unless God allows it to happen. If God allows something to happen, good or bad, it's because God knows the heart and what's best for a human.

God knows how to use anything and everything to save souls. As long as humans are fearing him, and praying that God uses each and everything that they can possibly go through to glorify his name. The fear of the Lord is key to staying away from all the evil that is in the world, while at the same time, it gives the ability to love those who are of the world even when they are not doing the right things.

Hebrew 13: 1 – 9 says:

> Let brotherly love continue.
>
> Be not forgetful to entertain strangers: for thereby some
>
> have entertained angels unawares.
>
> Remember them that are in bonds, as bound with them;
>
> and them which suffer adversity, as being yourselves
>
> also in the body.
>
> Marriage is honorable in all, and the bed undefiled:
>
> but whoremongers and adulterers God will judge.
>
> Let your conversation be without covetousness; and be content
>
> with such things as ye have: for he hath said, I will never leave thee,
>
> no forsake thee.
>
> So that we may boldly say, the lord is my helper, and I will not
>
> fear what man shall do unto me.
>
> Remember them which have the rule over you, who have spoken
>
> unto you the word of God: whose faith follow,
>
> considering the end of their conversation.
>
> Jesus Christ the same yesterday and today, and forever.
>
> Be not carried about with divers and strange doctrines.
>
> For it is a good thing that the heart be established with grace;
>
> not with meat, which have not profited them that have been occupied therein.

Chapter 14

Comfort from the Lord

2 Corinthians 1: 2 – 6 says:

Grace be to you and peace from God our Father,

and from the Lord Jesus Christ.

Blessed be God, even the Father of our Lord Jesus Christ,

the Father of mercies, and the God of all comfort; who comforteth

us in all our tribulation, that we may be able to comfort them

which are in any trouble, by the comfort wherewith we

ourselves are comforted of God.

For as the sufferings of Christ abound in us, so our consolation

also aboundeth by Christ.

And whether we be afflicted, it is for your consolation and

salvation, which is effectual in the enduring of the same

sufferings which we also suffer: or whether we be comforted,

it is for your consolation and salvation.

There will always be hard and painful times in life, whether it's being locked away, losing a close family member, a job, a friend or maybe even losing physical ability, due to being in some kind of accident. If enduring a tragic moment in life, the best things a human can do in life is seek God for comfort and strength to carry on. Not only will the Lord give humans comfort because Jesus has already been through in life, but God will use a human and their situations to comfort others that may not truly have a relationship with Jesus Christ. This is so they can receive the message that Christ is the comforter of all comforters.

How can a human seek God for comfort? They can simply trust in the word of God, which is the Bible and lean not on their own understanding when times get rough. When times do get rough humans must press into the truth, so they can allow God to bring them the victory. In doing so humans begin to be engulfed in the fruits of the Spirit, which are, love, Joy, peace, faith, goodness, gentleness, meekness, and long-suffering.

When humans are walking in the Spirit, the Spirit rises above the flesh, and that brings forth a stillness to any storm that a human my face in life. Storms in a human's life can be their emotions rising, a bad situation, it can be another person's childish ways. It can be lust, envy, and many other things that humans tend to struggle with in life.

In the gospel of Luke 8: 22 – 25, it says:

> Now it came to pass on a certain day, that he went into a ship
> with his disciples: and he said unto them, let us go over unto the
> other side of the lake.
> And they launched forth.
> But as they sailed he fell asleep: and there came down a
> storm of wind on the lake: and they were filled with water,
> and were in jeopardy.
> And they came to him, and awoke him, saying, 'Master, master,
> we perish.
> 'Then he arose, and rebuked the wind and the raging of the water:

and they ceased, and there was a calm.

And he said unto them, where is your faith? And they being

afraid wondered, saying one to another, what manner of man is this!

For he commandeth even the winds and water, and they obey him.

As humans it's an everyday job to call on Jesus Christ to handle the situation when the storms of life begin to rage. Not only should humans call on Jesus Christ. They must also have faith, by sitting still to allow Jesus Christ the chance to calm the storms that are raging in their life. When doing these things, god's promises are sure to come, and God will be that comforter of all comforters, whom each and every human truly needs in their life.

Matthew 5: 4 says, "Blessed are they that mourn: for they shall be comforted."

Giving Praise

Psalm 63: 1 – 8 says:

O God, thou art my God; early will I seek thee: my soul

thirsteth for thee, my flesh longeth for thee in a dry and thirsty

land, where no water is; to see thy power and thy glory,

so as I have seen thee in the sanctuary.

Because thy loving kindness is better than life, my lips shall praise thee.

Thus will I bless thee while I live: I will lift up my hands in thy name.

My soul shall be satisfied as with marrow and fatness; and my

mouth shall praise thee with joyful lips: when I remember thee

upon my bed, and meditate on thee in the night watches.

Because thou hast been my help, therefore in the shadow

      of thy wings will I rejoice.

My soul followeth hard after thee: thy right hand upholdeth me.

    The book of Psalms was written by David, a servant of God who continually praised the Lord with his words and actions, which is why the Psalms are full of praises to God. It is very important to thank God and give him praise for everything. It does not make a difference if the situation is good, bad, or ugly, even if it's something a human does not like, they should give God praise for bringing them through, even if a humans is still in the middle of that situation, because God is the author and finisher of everything that is and is to come.

    It's also important for a human to understand that God is truly good all the time. In Romans 8: 28, the word of God states, "And we know that all things work together for good to them that love God, to them that are called according to his purpose. "Then in Romans 8:31, the word of God state, "What shall we then say to these things? If God be for us who can be against us?"

    When God has spoken these kinds of things to all humans, then why in the world would they not want to praise the Lord's name for each and everything that happens in life? And not just for what happens, but for every second Christ lives within them, while building them into whom God created them to be.

    By truly giving God the praise for everything, humans further their relationship with Christ. They begin to understand the amount of suffering he went through for the forgiveness of all sins. Not only will a person's relationship grow with Christ, but they will truly be blessed for standing in the will of God by simply giving themselves as a living sacrifice to God for Christ to live through.

In the word of God, Galatians 2:20 says, "I am crucified with Christ: nevertheless I live; yet not I, but Christ liveth in me: and the life which I now live in the flesh I live by the faith of the Son of God, who loved me, and gave himself for me. "Paul, who truly received a true relationship with Jesus Christ, through faith, was used by the Spirit of God to write the book of Galatians. Paul truly expresses how important it is to deny self, so that Christ can live.

If humans had enough faith and trust to do the things which Paul speaks throughout the Epistles the Holy Spirit used him to write, they would allow Christ to carry them out of the flesh and through the spiritual realm. Just like Paul did they would be surrendering all to God.

In the flesh Paul was a man who persecuted the Jews and it was Christ who softened up Paul's heart to love the way that God made him to love. In doing so Christ turned Paul 108 degrees form the man that he used to be, and into the man that he was meant to be. In giving God the praise through everything, humans can do nothing except allow Christ to live through them. If they are doing so, they are glorifying God's name.

Psalm 145: 8 – 15 says:

> The Lord is gracious, and full of compassion; slow to anger,
>> and of great mercy.
> The Lord is good to all: and his tender mercies are over all his works.
> All thy works shall praise thee, O Lord; and they saints shall bless thee.

They shall speak of the glory of thy kingdom, and talk of thy power;

To make known to the sons of men his mighty acts, and the

glorious majesty of his kingdom.

Thy kingdom is an everlasting kingdom, and thy dominion endureth

throughout all generations.

The Lord upholdeth all that fall, and raiseth up all that bowed down.

The eyes of all wait upon thee; and thou givest them their meat in due

season.

Chapter 15

The Healing of the Lord

2 Kings 20: 4 – 8 says:

> And it came to pass, afore Isaiah was gone out into the middle
> court, that the word of the Lord came to him, saying,
> 'Turn again, and tell Hezekiah the captain of my people,
> thus saith the Lord, the God of David they father, I have heard
> thy prayer, I have seen thy tears: behold I will heal thee: on the
> third day thou shalt go up unto the house of the Lord.
> And I will add unto thy days fifteen years; and I will deliver thee and
> this city out of the hand of the King of Assyria;
> and I will defend this city for mine own sake, and for my servant
> David's sake. '
> And Isaiah said, 'Take a lump of figs. 'And they took and laid it on the
> boil, and he recovered.
> And Hezekiah said unto Isaiah, 'What shall be the sign that the
> Lord will heal me, and that I shall go up into the house of the Lord the third
> day?'

God begins to heal a human's heart by first revealing to them that the things they think and do are wrong. It is just a part of human nature to do things wrong and not according to God's will. Having a heart for Christ is where the healing process begins.

When a human is facing a painful situation in life - - yes a painful situation, because those situations do pop up from time to time, throughout a human's life

-- a human should give any hurt they may have to God and ask him to heal the pain. In due time God will do what they have asked of him, because he hears the prayers of a broken and contrite heart.

A lot of the time, humans tends to run from God and right into worldly ways to get over painful situations, such as sex, drugs, hurting others and many more wrongful things. Humans must always keep faith that Jesus Christ is and will always be the only true overcomer of any situation that they can face in life. In Isaiah 53:5, it says, "But he was wounded for our transgressions, he was bruised for our iniquities; the chastisement of our peace was upon him; and with his stripes we are healed. "

Right there in God's word it speaks in large volumes about Jesus Christ taking the stripes across his back to heal the pain caused by the sinful nature of humankind. Every single lashing that Jesus Christ took was a sign of healing for each and every human's painful sins. When it's all said and done when a human sins they do nothing, but bring pain to themselves.

Part of the reason why Jesus Christ went through everything that he went through was so that humans could be healed. The only way humans can truly be healed is by giving their pain to God. This way God can use it to save many souls that may be going through pain due to holding onto worldly things by removing the veil that is over the spiritual eyes of many humans who are lost in worldly ways.

Not that followers of Jesus Christ are any better than those who are not following Jesus Christ, because every single human falls short of God's glory daily no matter how good of a person they try to be. It's more about spiritual eyes being open, because with Jesus Christ the world is made a better place. The more humans there are that fight the good fight, the more God can heal and bless all humankind.

Jesus Christ has already healed the pain of many rape victims, rapists, abused children, killers, and also the pain of anyone who has been close to someone who has been a victim to or has done such things. Every human who may be involved or even around something like that is also a victim of the pain it may cause, no matter if they admit to it or not.

There are many things humans go through, or have been through in life, that they have never spoken about. Most people don't want to hear about it or most likely they won't believe it. But when a human holds those deep dark secrets in, it begins to cause more and more pain in their life. And until a human can truly give those deep dark secrets to Jesus Christ without having fear that someone is going to get in trouble or hurt, is when they can truly give Jesus Christ the power to heal and save souls through them and their testimony.

As a man of God it's safe to say that it's not an easy thing to truly follow the ways of Jesus Christ, but the truth is that God's mercy endures forever. Because of that a human should never give up on God's will being done in their life. That way God's Glory will be shown through the love he has for humankind.

This is the very reason why believers go through things in life, then they turn the situation around for good by giving whatever it is to God, so that Jesus Christ can use it in a righteous manner and also bring that human through a tough situation. With Jesus Christ God is giving them flavor, which makes them the salt of the earth. But that is only because of the test which God allowed them to go through. Matthew 5:13 says, "ye are the salt of the earth: but if the salt has lost its savor, wherewith shall it be salted? It is thenceforth good for nothing, but to be cast out, and to be trodden underfoot of man."

This is the very reason why a believer's test becomes their testimony of what Jesus Christ has brought them through. The healing process is a miracle all in itself. When humans look in the word of God and read through the Gospels, they will see the miracles of healing which God did through the prayers of Jesus Christ in the flesh. God still does those miracles through human believers for the other humans as long as they ask through prayer in the name of Jesus Christ.

Through the spiritual eyes God has revealed his truth healing the soul through the stories of Jesus Christ healing the lame, the blind, the dead rising, and the sleeping being awoke. When humans are lost in the world and caught up in all the worldly ways, plus they think that they are doing everything right. It only means they are blind to the truth, they are dead in their sins, laid up in their own ways or might have what the word of God sometimes calls leprosy, or another sickness. All in all they are sick of life, but through the spiritual eyes, when accepting Jesus Christ in their heart by allowing Christ to live through them, it allows God to begin healing the things that have hurt a person in their past. When that happens, they become raised from the death of sin. The veil gets removed from their spiritual eyes so that they can truly understand the way that God work's and they will start to understand how good God really is.

Matthew 8: 14 – 17 says:

> And when Jesus was come into Peter's house, he saw his wife's
> mother laid, and sick of a fever.

And he touched her hand, and the fever left her: and she arose,

and ministered unto them.

When the evening was come, they brought unto him many that

were possessed with devils: and he cast out the spirits with his

word, and healed all that were sick:

That it might be fulfilled which was spoken by Esaias the prophet,

saying, himself took our infirmities, and bear our sickness.

In the name of Jesus be healed!

Chapter 16

Vengeance Is the Lord's

Matthew 5: 43 – 48 says:

> Ye have heard that it hast been said, thou shalt love thy neighbor,
>> and hate thine enemy.
> But I say unto you, love your enemies, bless them that curse you,
>> do good to them that hate you, and pray for them which
>> despitefully use you, and persecute you;
> That ye may be the children of your father which is in heaven:
>> for he maketh his sun to rise on the evil and on the good,
>> and sendeth rain on the just and on the unjust.
> For if ye love them which love you, what reward have ye?
> Do not even the publicans the same?
> And if ye salute your brethren only, what do ye more than others?
>> Do not even publicans so?
> Be ye therefore perfect, even as your father which is in heaven is perfect.

In life humans tend to reap what they sow. There are times in life when a human can be doing all that he or she can to do the right things with their life, but yet it is as If every one of the world is working against them doing the right things. Sometimes it's not only the world, but even by those who are in the church.

A lot of humans tend to live their life, being used by the adversary to stop another human from living life righteously by living their life as Jesus Christ lives his. When humans are done wrong by another human, they should pray and leave it in God's hands. When they are doing that, they begin to stand strong in the armor of God, which was spoken about in the end of Chapter 7 of this book.

The Lord's vengeance is very merciful and this is why: it's because a lot of times when believers get done wrong, or should I say persecuted for righteousness' sake by another individual, it's usually because the other individual is not able to see or understand the way, the truth, and the life. In John 14:6 the word of God says, "Jesus saith unto him, 'I am the way, the truth, and the life: no man cometh to the father, but by me.' "The word clearly speaks of Jesus Christ as being the way, truth, and life. But it is up to humans if they are going to truly accept that truth in their life or not. The only way they can really receive that truth in their life is by following Jesus Christ. When individuals are persecuting other individuals who are following Jesus Christ, the Lord begins to do what he does to remove the veil from the individuals the chance to begin a real-life relationship with Jesus Christ. The individuals who were persecuting those who were following Jesus Christ will begin to slowly open their spiritual eyes so that they can begin seeing things the way that God does.

Once God begins a work in a human's life, he will see to it that his work is finished, no matter what happens. It's because of the work that God started on humankind that Jesus Christ is continually at the door of a human's heart constantly knocking with hope that they will open up. A lot of times , humans never truly open the door of their heart to let Jesus Christ in and when a human does not open up to let Jesus Christ in, they begin to shut out the blessings which God has promised them from the beginning of time and for all the time to come, generation after generation.

Not only would a human miss out on their blessings if they continue to walk against God's will, but they can also be cursed to the point of God removing his hands off of their life by allowing the enemy to devour them. In doing so, humans become a slave to sin instead of being a friend and servant of Jesus Christ. If humans become slaves to sin it is because they are giving Satan control. If they are giving Satan control, that means that Satan along with his little principalities of darkness have the chance to steal, kill, and destroy.

God himself is protector of all that kind of stuff and there are angels ready to go to war for the saints against the adversary along with all the other evil spirits. One thing is sure, when everything is said and done the word of God states that every knee will bow and that every tongue will confess that Jesus Christ, the Son of God, is Lord forever. Everything else does not matter because there is just no way around that.

Revelation 12: 7 – 12 says:

And there was a war in heaven: Michael and his angels fought

against the dragon; and the dragon fought and his angels,

and prevailed not; neither was their place found any

more in heaven.

And the great dragon was cast out, that old serpent, called the devil,

and Satan, which deceiveth the whole world: he was cast out

into the earth, and his angels were cast out with him.

And I heard a loud voice saying in heaven, now is come salvation,

and strength, and the kingdom of our God, and the power

of his Christ: for the accuser of our brothren is cast down,

which accused them before our God day and night.

And they overcome him by the blood of the lamb, and by the word of their testimony; and they loved not their lives unto the death.

Rejoice, ye heavens, and ye that dwell in them.

Woe to the inhabiters of the earth and the sea!

For the devil is come down unto you, having great worth, because he knoweth that he hath but a short time.

Chapter 17

God Take Control of my Everyday Fight

I pray, God, take control. Fight this fight for me. There have been ups and downs in my everyday walk with you, but your word in Exodus 14:14 tells me, "The Lord shall fight for you, and ye shall hold your peace."

Well, Lord, by all means I am sitting still, but I am angry. My flesh wants so bad to use violence to overcome those who have done wrong to me. I am trapped in the punishment that their lies have trumped up against me. Yet it's no longer my fight. I give it to you and I pray that you finish the forgiveness in my heart. I also pray that you forgive those who continually rise against me daily to try keeping me stuck in my past. It's no longer I who lives but it's your Son who lives within me.

I understand that this fight is not against flesh and blood, it's against principalities and darkness, but, Lord, those who are walking in the flesh continue to rise up against me. Or not me, but you, because it's I who walks in you and it's you who walks through me. How much longer will those around me be able to keep a hold on the life that you have given me? It's been 8 long years and I ask that your will is to free me from this trap.

I continually fall short of your glory. I continue to bump heads with those around me who have no faith in you. I stay to myself from time to time because I love to speak of you and most people think that I am crazy for believing in you as my lord and Savior. Not that it matters what others think, because my soul is truly yours, but that is just the truth of the matter.

In their eyes I am standing for you but I am still locked away with them. It's as if they have no reason to seek after you. Yet they continue to fall into the lies of the world by trying to build a profile of worldly certificates to convince man that they have changed because of these worldly classes they take. But the truth is that the foundation cannot be worldly, it must be you, because you are the rock, the foundation that will not be moved even when the storms of life arise.

You speak of this foundation in Luke 6: 48 – 49:

> He is like a man which built an house, and digged deep,
>> and laid the foundation on a rock: and when the flood arose,
>> the stream beat vehemently upon that house, and could
>> not shake it: for it was founded upon a rock.
> But he that hearteth, and doeth not is like a man that without
>> a foundation built an house upon the earth; against which
>> the stream did beat vehemently, and immediately it fell;
>> and the ruin of the house was great.

Not only did you speak of the house being built on you and what happens when the storms of life arise, but you also spoke of the worldly foundation. You let it be known that it will be wiped away when the storms arise.

Lord, are they stuck in worldly ways because they choose not to read your word? Have they read your word and disregarded it? Lord what is it? Why can they not see that it's you who is the way to heaven and out of the mess that they have been living in?

There are many things I do not agree with in this world, but I do agree with you. Because of that, my soul continues to grow every step of the way. It's because of you; your will, mercy, grace and forgiveness that I have had my eyes open to the truth. I see all the lies and I understand that the only truth in this world is you and your words. I understand that the devil is the father of lies and that God is my Father, the Father of truth.

When the world pushes their lies at me, your word helps me overcome. Your Holy Spirit raises me above the lie and sets me in your truth. Well, here I am Lord, not perfect, but without blemish because of your will being done in my life. I ask that you continue to heal me from the hurt that I have and will endure while following you to the best of my ability. I know it's not about what I do, but about what you have done.

Lord, as you know, I have been asking if you can use me for anything and I continually ask that you use me with every breath that I take for the rest of my life and for all eternity.

The End

Prayers

To Be Born Again

Lord, I have lived my life in a way I thought was right. I understand now that I need you in my life, so I ask that Jesus Christ comes into my heart, my life, and most importantly take control of me along with my actions. I pray for forgiveness of the things I have done against your will knowingly, and also for the things I have don't against your will without knowing.

God, you are my creator and I have faith in you along with all your ways. You have kept me safe all the way up unto this point in life and as long as I am here, I am yours to used. In the name of Jesus I pray.

Amen

A Backslider

Lord, I come to you this day in the name of Jesus, asking to be clothed in your robe of righteousness, covered in the blood of the Lamb. Forgive me for turning my back and walking away from you and your ways. I am back now because without you, Lord, I am nothing. Just like the story of the prodigal son, who left with his share of the riches and tried to live on his own, Lord, I have done the same and now I realize that I am in need of you. Lord, I thank you for keeping me safe and healthy; do with me as you wish, because you know what's best for me in Jesus name.

Amen.

About the Author

Marcus Thaddeus Clayton was born March 1st, 1987 at Tacoma General Hospital in Tacoma, WA. He graduated from Spanaway Lake High School in 2005. He had a Baptist upbringing and was baptized when he was about 8 years old. Although he fell into the wrong kind of life and made many bad choices, he found salvation through Jesus Christ. He shares the message that Christ saves all those who seek him – even those like Marcus, who fell away from Christ for a time -- through his writing. His writing was influenced by Joyce Meyer, the 70x7 series, and other nonfiction and urban fiction authors. He aspires to make a sacrifice of the rest of his life to help others. His writing is one outlet he has found for that calling.

I have known Marcus personally for years and can attest to his steadfast, unostentatious, humble faith in God and the positive effect it's had on his life. He is true to his word, reliable, and honest, which are not always easy qualities to maintain in the prison environment where he finds himself. He has confided in me the heartrending story of deep introspection and person questioning he underwent in the hole after he committed the crime for which he is currently in prison. He told me that he thought of family members he loves aging 30 years in his absence and how the only salvation he could find was through a positive relationship with God. He let God have his suffering, pain, and remorse, and committed himself to living his plan. Now, he is a true object of admiration throughout the system, doing what he can to foster positive change in others. I have found myself inspired by his great example.

He is currently in the process of putting together his autobiographical follow – up books. He knows he will receive his physical freedom when God feels he is ready, but he also know his spiritual freedom has already been given to him – through Christ.

Ed.

Made in the USA
Coppell, TX
20 March 2021